T0286879

Cambridge Elements ≡

Elements in Shakespeare Performance
edited by
W. B. Worthern
Barnard College

SHAKESPEARE'S VISIONARY WOMEN

Laura Jayne Wright
Newcastle University

CAMBRIDGE
UNIVERSITY PRESS

Shaftesbury Road, Cambridge CB2 8EA, United Kingdom

One Liberty Plaza, 20th Floor, New York, NY 10006, USA

477 Williamstown Road, Port Melbourne, VIC 3207, Australia

314–321, 3rd Floor, Plot 3, Splendor Forum, Jasola District Centre,
New Delhi – 110025, India

103 Penang Road, #05–06/07, Visioncrest Commercial, Singapore 238467

Cambridge University Press is part of Cambridge University Press & Assessment,
a department of the University of Cambridge.

We share the University's mission to contribute to society through the pursuit
of education, learning and research at the highest international levels of excellence.

www.cambridge.org
Information on this title: www.cambridge.org/9781009054911

DOI: 10.1017/9781009057394

First published 2023

A catalogue record for this publication is available from the British Library

ISBN 978-1-009-05491-1 Paperback
ISSN 2516-0117 (online)
ISSN 2516-0109 (print)

Shakespeare's Visionary Women

Elements in Shakespeare Performance

DOI: 10.1017/9781009057394

First published online: November 2023

Laura Jayne Wright

Newcastle University

Author for correspondence: Laura Jayne Wright, Laura.wright2@newcastle.ac.uk

ABSTRACT: Shakespeare's visionary women, usually confined to the periphery, claim centre stage to voice their sleeping and waking dreams. These women recount their visions through acts of rhetoric, designed to persuade and, crucially, to directly intervene in political action. The visions discussed in this Element are therefore not simply moments of inspiration but of political intercession. The vision performed or recounted on stage offers a proleptic moment of female speech that forces audiences to confront questions of narrative truth and women's testimony. This Element interrogates the scepticism that Shakespeare's visionary women face and considers the ways in which they perform the truth of their experiences to a hostile onstage audience. It concludes that prophecy gives women a brief moment of access to political conversations in which they are not welcome as they wrest narrative control from male speakers and speak their truth aloud.

This Element also has a video abstract: www.Cambridge.org/Wright

KEYWORDS: Shakespeare, visions, women, sight, future

ISBNs: 9781009054911 (PB), 9781009057394 (OC)

ISSNs: 2516-0117 (online), 2516-0109 (print)

Contents

Author's Note

All primary quotations drawn from unedited early modern texts have been modernised and their orthography standardised throughout. However, primary quotations drawn from modern editions retain the style of that edition. Titles of primary works take modernised and abridged form in my prose but can be found in full in my bibliography. Speech prefixes in drama extracts have been presented in a uniform style. Where it has not been possible to cite line numbers, page numbers or signature marks are given. All references to Shakespeare are taken from *The Oxford Shakespeare: The Complete Works*, ed. John Jowett, William Montgomery, Gary Taylor, and Stanley Wells (Oxford: Oxford University Press, 1986; 2005), unless otherwise specified. All references to Shakespeare's First Folio (1623) are to the digital facsimile of the Bodleian First Folio of Shakespeare's plays, Arch. G c.7, accessed at firstfolio.bodleian.ox.ac.uk/. All Bible references are to the King James Version.

1 Introduction: Given to Lie

> a very honest woman, but something given to lie.
>
> (*Antony and Cleopatra*, 5.2.246–47)

Honest, but given to lie. This paradox, spoken by a Clown and suggesting in a wry line the doubtful value of capricious female testimony, might serve to summarise the position of visionary women in Shakespeare's dramatic works. Shakespeare's playworlds are full of premonitions, pointed dreams, and prophetic declarations. His characters are often intuitive, from Venus who warns Adonis, 'I prophesy thy death, my living sorrow' (666) to Juliet, whose 'ill-divining soul' prompts her to see Romeo 'As one dead at the bottom of a tomb' (3.5.54–6). While many such moments suggest that women are highly perceptive, if not even able to see the future, it is with the particular nuances of women's *political* prophecy that I am concerned here. This is an examination not only of female experience but also of female speech. The visionaries I discuss must make their ineffable experiences effable in order to change the outcome of political decisions. Claiming divine inspiration, extrasensory instinct, or magical influence, these women recount their visions in acts of rhetoric, designed not only to satisfy sceptical male hearers but to make them take action.[1] The political visions discussed here are not only moments of inspiration but of intercession. The success of a vision depends on how persuasive visionary women are able to be in recounting it: belief in a vision comes down to the power of the visionary as orator more than oracle.

The political vision breaches the accepted sphere of female speech. Women speak on matters of both a political and (for their husbands and brothers) a personal future, participating in such discussions through their words of warning and often invoking the claim of divine or supernatural inspiration as both authority and excuse. The eight visionary women discussed in this Element intervene in political conversations to which they are, to differing degrees, denied access, not least because 'women were not supposed to have a *public* voice, much less a public *political* voice' (Schwoerer, 1998: 56).[2] The default reaction visionary women face from their hearers is doubt. This is not to say that all women who share visions on the Shakespearean stage are disbelieved (or that all visionary men are automatically given credence, as Lear's Fool and Caesar's soothsayer find out), but when women are believed it is *in spite* of the assumption that they are liars or lunatics. The politically charged prophecies of the characters discussed here, when brought together, offer an overwhelming pattern, even a dramatic type. The political visionary, endowed with supernatural knowledge beyond her own, apparently limited, understanding, can offer essential political insight, should the men around her be astute enough to follow it: she is not only a harbinger of doom but a forward-thinking advisor who can

---

[1] While onstage women tend to describe their visions to men, their offstage audience, of course, also comprised women (Levin, 1989: 165–74). It is also necessary to note that the roles described here were all played by men, adding a further complication to the representation of female speech and agency.

[2] Following Lois G. Schwoerer, I largely use 'political' or 'political culture' rather than 'politics': the term intends to capture the broader ways in which women of all classes might participate in the power structures around them including, importantly for this study, 'influencing decision makers' and 'petitioning' (1998: 57).

influence men to act on her vision's warning. The following study is therefore also a study of women witnessing: the fundamental question of a visionary experience – *do you see what I see?* – splinters the received reality of a play and in that splintering makes space for further questions of misogyny, faith, and political intercession.

Shakespeare wrote within a culture that allowed, theoretically, for visionary women. Prophetesses, soothsayers, wise women, and witches were familiar, not only as figures in literature or in religious texts, but as figures of both recent history and present-day controversy. Classical mythology offered plentiful examples of divine and divinely inspired seers, from the Sibyl at Cumae to the Oracle at Delphi, the Parcae to Cassandra. The Old Testament acknowledges that some women speak the word of God (such as Miriam and Deborah). The New Testament offers the Virgin Mary's encounter with Gabriel and names Mary Magdalene as witness to the Resurrection. Yet, despite these precedents, contemporary prophecies were often treated as highly threatening, especially when invoked as political tools: '"prophecies of one kind or another were employed in virtually every rebellion or popular rising which disturbed the Tudor state", and Henry VIII, Edward VI and Elizabeth I all found it necessary to legislate against them' (Hobday, 1979: 72). Whenever they appear in his work, Shakespeare makes clear that political visionary women are dangerous; in fact, the following sections show consistent punishment for visionary women who speak of or to power. Yet, on the other hand, Shakespeare makes clear that those visionary women speak the truth. It is a contradiction that is never resolved, playing out again and again across Shakespeare's work. Shakespeare's visionary women emerge as articulate political thinkers stifled by disbelief, condemned for their capacity to see the future, dismissed for their dreams.

The women in Shakespeare's plays who experience visions or apparitions not only face the difficulty of speaking up in a patriarchal society, but of articulating their inner sight without retaliatory accusations of witchcraft, madness, or hysteria. Their thoughts, dreams, and instincts are necessarily performed for a judging audience. This is therefore an examination not only of extrasensory experiences and how those experiences are staged, but also of authority and agency, and – because these women are not only passive advisors or intercessors – of personal ambition. That ambition and agency must be considered in all its complexity; while all of Shakespeare's women speak within a patriarchal system, their circumstances are various and distinct. In *1 Henry VI*, Joan moves with the authority of the biblical prophetesses she invokes as ancestors but has no earthly connections to call upon when accused of witchcraft. Cassandra is dismissed as mad but is also able to access the centre of the Trojan court through her father, King Priam. Katherine of Aragon, an ex-queen whose royal privilege is now failing, can be held against those freshly aspiring to royal power, such as Eleanor and Lady Macbeth. These women speak from different positions of power: their visionary experiences, or more precisely their experiences of testifying to their own visions, are therefore different. What these women have in common, however, is that very act of public testifying, and the limited contingency of the belief which they are extended.

This contingency is neatly captured by Shakespeare's perhaps best-known visionary women, the witches of *Macbeth*. The witches offer only balanced contradictions ('Fair is foul, and foul is fair', 1.1.10) that equate prophecy with fallacy: if foul is fair, then all semantic distinctions are lost and anything and its opposite could be true. This contradiction is also evident in their decision to meet 'When the battle's lost and won' (1.1.4). That prophecy is at once easily proved true (they reappear, as of course the dramatist can ensure, at the end of the battle) and impossible to prove (if the battle is won by Macbeth, it will not be 'ere the set of sun', 5: that victory won't be apparent until after he has killed Duncan). It is also a logical redundancy: if someone has lost a battle, someone has won it. Yet, despite this contradiction, the witches are alone amongst the visionaries discussed here in being believed without question. The reason for this is simple. It is not because there are three witches, able to corroborate each other's visions (after all, as I discuss in Section 2, Cassandra and Andromache speak together). It is not because they have any demonstrable magic powers: Macbeth and Banquo only encounter three women on the heath.[3] It is rather,

---

[3] Complicating this description, Orgel discusses the 'beards' of the witches and the ways in which 'The specifically and dangerously female here expresses itself through masculine attributes' (1996: 110). The witches (as I also discussed in the case of Joan in Section 4) are condemned by misogynistic expectations of gender which damn them for being female and not being female enough: 'Witches,

uninspiringly, because their prophecy is favourable: the Macbeths both hear what they want to hear, their own ambitions resounding as if in an echo chamber. The witches both demonstrate the role of prophecy as a means for women to speak, however obscurely, on politics, and also that the chances of that prophecy being believed is contingent not only on the scepticism with which women's voices are met, but on the content of the prophecy itself: it is easier to persuade someone who is already inclined to agree, as the many visionary women discussed in the following often find out.

Negotiating the boundaries of their domestic roles, visionary women at once intervene in the public political culture of the court and speak in private settings of their dreams, worries, and hopes for their husband's future and, by extension, their own. An ideal wife should, after all, advise her husband, although only in appropriate settings. She might offer a 'curtain lecture', a term that Neil Rhodes has shown was used widely in the period to describe private moments of intercession in which a wife would advise her husband on his affairs within the closed-off space of their bed (2020: 111–12). Yet, the 'lectures' with which I am concerned are often public speeches and often closer to instructions than to guidance: they are not moments of intimate, deferential advice offered when it is decorous to do so. The New Testament offers the model of this conversation: Pilate's wife, recounts a dream to warn against the execution of Jesus. The incident is contained within a single verse, which suggests a public moment of intercession: 'When he was set down on the judgment seat, his wife sent unto him, saying, Have thou nothing to do with that just man: for I have suffered many things this day in a dream because of him' (Matthew 27:19).

There is no explanation in Matthew for the visionary dream. The narrative moves immediately to the persuasive arguments of the chief priests and elders, who convince Pilate to secure Barabbas's rather than Jesus's release. The account is so brief that various renditions in medieval and early modern literature must supplement it and therefore differ wildly as to the origin of the dream. On stage, in the Tapiters and Couchers' play of the York Mystery

though epitomizing what was conceived as a specifically female propensity to wickedness, were also regularly accused of being either unfeminine or androgynous' (110).

cycle, the dream's aetiology is unambiguous: Lucifer whispers in the ear of 'Sir Pilate's witless wife' as she sleeps (Poulton, 2016: 89). Yet, in *Salve Deus Rex Judaeorum* (1611), Aemilia Lanyer frames the dream as a divine warning. Lanyer's narrator addresses Pilate directly: 'But hear the words of thy most worthy wife, / Who sends to thee, to beg her Saviours life' (Lanyer, 1611: C4 v). It is Pilate who lacks vision: 'Open thine eyes, that thou the truth may'st see', Lanyer's narrator demands. Pilate's wife's dream offers a precedent for several of the concerns that play out in Shakespeare's representation of visionaries onstage. The first is the possibility of ascribing two entirely contradictory origins – divine and demonic – to a vision. The second is the lack of acknowledgement given to female visionaries even when their prophecies are ultimately proved true. The New Testament offers no response to Pilate's wife; if Pilate answered, readers are not given that answer. Many of the visionaries I discuss follow Pilate's wife's not only in standing as a public witness to their own dreams, but also in receiving no fair answer or being dismissed from the narrative. This is the paradox of visionary women: they claim a rare opportunity to speak publicly and yet are swiftly silenced.

Shakespeare's visionary women must share their visions in front of an audience, even if they seek privacy. The stage is a space where the act of witnessing is publicly performed and publicly inspected, a platform on which women recount personal, internalised experiences. The stage puts the account of the vision up for public judgement and forces its truth to be confronted, whether or not that vision is actually shown to the audience. The vision itself can be an absent theatrical experience, taking place offstage. In considering such visions, I am indebted to Andrew Sofer's concept of theatrical 'dark matter', 'the invisible dimension of theater that escapes visual detection, even though its effects are felt everywhere in performance' as the play 'incorporates the incorporeal' (Sofer, 2013: 3). Sofer explicitly names hallucinations (not easily distinguished from prophetic experiences) amongst these 'invisible presences', drifting onstage when they have been dreamed within, discussed in passing, reported second-hand. Without seeing it for oneself, it is impossible to verify a vision, not least because the visions discussed here are not shared (as, say, Hamlet's encounter with his father's ghost is supported by Horatio). Women usually experience visions alone and, even in rare cases such as that of Andromache and

Cassandra, discussed below, the sight of a particular vision or manifestation itself is not shared. The exception to that rule lies with the audience: although visions are often intangible dark matter there are moments (as discussed in Section 4) in which playgoers share a vision with the visionary woman, forced into the complicated role of potential corroborators who see what the visionary sees but must nonetheless remain silent.

Yet, despite the various doubts and prejudiced outlined here, the scenes examined below do not suggest that for women to speak up in matters of political culture is entirely fruitless; even when they are dismissed, they do, for a moment, model the act of political intervention and do so before an audience. For women in Shakespeare (as in the early modern courtroom), the act of bearing witness was an act of claiming the floor, however briefly. Laura Gowing describes giving testimony in the early modern courtroom as a kind of performance: 'For women, witnessing also involved a shift that put them at the centre of dramas of sex, words, and marriage ... The act of testifying gave a weight to women's words and an attention to women's points of view that was rarely accorded them in law or in culture' (Gowing, 1996: 234).

In a transition that Gowing describes as a move from 'bystander to actor', women took control of their own narrative for as long as they held the floor to testify to it. Gowing's work also offers a model for understanding the performance of witnessing on the stage. Although the Shakespearean characters described in these pages do not testify in court (as, say, Hermione is made to do in *The Winter's Tale*), they nonetheless claim stage space for the brief time it takes to narrate their visions. Yet, unlike the women Gowing describes as offering legal testimony, which is predicated on the truth of tangible experience, visionary women are compelled to narrate experiences that they themselves cannot be sure are true. Therefore, this work is not concerned with lived experience so much as with the *un-lived*, unshared experience of sights that are real and accessible only to the visionary herself and are shared by her for the purpose of inciting change.

Women in Shakespeare's plays are frequently portrayed as having access to foreknowledge or divine knowledge, especially in Shakespeare's tragedies and histories, genres that are predicated on the temporal structures of what has been (history) and what will be (tragic fate). The power and scope of these visions unsettles not only the balance of knowledge which is assumed to be held by men but the reality of the worlds being constructed before an audience's eyes. In my account of visionary women, I begin with two women who have prophetic dreams within the context of Trojan and Roman cultures that at least appear sympathetic to omens and augury: Calphurnia and Cassandra. Both characters, as I will discuss, articulate their dreams with precision, only to be dismissed by the very men their prophecies concern. I then turn to characters whose visions are more firmly associated both with their own apparently damaged psyches and with a culture of witchcraft: Lady Macbeth and Eleanor, Duchess of Gloucester. My next section is concerned with the representation of two historic women, Joan of Arc and Katherine of Aragon, women who see apparitions rather than abstract dreams. I finally consider the more slippery sensory experiences of Margaret of Anjou and Constance, both of whom describe sights that lie somewhere between imagination and vision. Together, this survey of visionary women suggests different but interwoven ways in which visionary women seek to claim space in political conversations. The vision offers a moment of knowledge and the possibility of agency: seeing beyond the earthly, visionaries use their experiences to actively intercede in their own political cultures.

The scenes discussed here offer examples of when and why women are believed (however fleetingly), what the role of a sceptical or supportive male auditor can offer, and how female-voiced visions contradict or confirm the predispositions of the men who hear them. The vision offers intervention but cannot always incite action: it is the description of a road not taken, a glimpse of another potential future that is soon cut short. Through sharing visions, visionary women onstage open themselves up to the particular vulnerability of becoming a spectacle: the question *do you see what I see?* becomes *do you see me?*

1.1 Believe Women: A Methodology

The vision on stage claims a strange temporal position, existing as it does in the past, present, and future. Shakespeare's visionary women, even those drawn from history, speak their own destinies aloud, in their present moment. Cleopatra, for instance, imagines a fate in which her life is treated as the subject of a comedy. In describing her prediction, Cleopatra invokes the language of the vision itself: 'I shall see / Some squeaking Cleopatra boy my greatness' (5.2.215–16), she claims, imagining not only a performance of herself, but herself as witness to it. Her words prove prophetic and, shifting from verb to noun, the Cleopatra player who 'boys' her greatness is in fact a squeaking boy actor on the seventeenth-century stage. This means that Cleopatra not only sees the future but also embodies it, as that very boy actor: her words 'shall see' become true in the present even as she speaks them aloud. The historical past of Cleopatra's life, the present of the early modern boy actor, and the future of her prediction fuse together in a time-bending moment that is typical of Shakespearean prophecies.[4] The visionaries discussed here frame the present through an understanding of the past and through thoughts of the future, living all three moments at once.

This text takes a similar approach to time in its own theoretical approach, understanding the vision both in a specific historic context and turning, whenever it is illuminating, to contemporary moments of performance that complicate and challenge such historicist readings. After all, Shakespeare's visionary scenes may reveal the alterity of early modern culture to our own contemporary playgoers, but they also demonstrate an 'aural misogyny' (Panjwani, 2022: 18) which is uncomfortably close to our present.[5] My own desire to examine the visionary experiences of the female characters discussed in these pages has certainly been shaped by contemporary cultural conversations about the position of women as testifiers of their own experiences and I want briefly to acknowledge that work. In *Tainted Witness: Why We Doubt What Women Say About Their Lives*, Leigh Gilmore aims to redress the fact that 'women's witness is discredited by a host of means meant to taint it: to

---

[4] In an article on Shakespeare and Fletcher's *Henry VIII*, I discuss the role of prophecies which 'predict' a future that has, for audiences, already passed using the neurological term, 'future-oriented mental time travel' (FMTT): see Wright (2021). The experience of hearing prophecy in *Henry VIII* as memory 're-written' is discussed by Hester Lees-Jeffries (2013), p. 89, and Susan Frye (2016), pp. 112–30.

[5] This is Varsha Panjwani's term, used in *Podcasts and Feminist Shakespeare Pedagogy*, in particular reference to *Hamlet* and *The Winter's Tale*. In her Element, Panjwani draws a connection between early modern culture and the way in which Shakespeare Studies itself 'sidelines the voices of women scholars' (18).

contaminate by doubt, stigmatize through association with gender and race, and dishonor through shame, such that not only the testimony but the person herself is smeared' (Gilmore, 2017: 2). While it would be disingenuous to compare the accounts of actual sexual violence that Gilmore discusses to the intangible, if often traumatic, visions of Shakespeare's female characters, what unites both is the position of assumed falsehood against which women speak.

Resistance to this bias has recently been given a simple, unifying motto, one which might as easily be applied to Shakespeare's stage as to the courtrooms of the United States for which it was coined. That motto, 'Believe Women', emerged from the MeToo movement, which was founded in 2006 by Tarana Burke, and in response to the 2018 Kavanaugh hearings. This motto has itself been subject to scepticism and interrogation, prompting a clarifying response from Jude Ellison Sady Doyle, 'Despite What You May Have Heard, "Believe Women" Has Never Meant "Ignore Facts"': 'The phrase is 'believe women' – meaning, don't assume women as a gender are especially deceptive or vindictive, and recognize that false allegations are less common than real ones' (Doyle, 2017). What Doyle articulates is not, of course, that women are infallible, but that when women offer testimony, they speak in the face of default disbelief. This scenario – a woman describing her own sensory experience to a hostile male audience – unfolds with such frustrating regularity across Shakespeare's plays that this Element might as easily have been called #BelieveShakespeare's Women.

The difficulty women face in being believed is, however, hardly a modern phenomenon. As Richards and Thorne discuss in their work on rhetoric, women, and politics in the early modern period, 'female petitioning was frequently met with ridicule and hostility' (2007: 1–2). Yet, while ridicule and hostility are certainly common reactions, the visions discussed here are staged as bravura performances of female eloquence if not, always, successful persuasion. The visionary women here are insistent and unapologetic, modelling the possibility of female political speech for female playgoers while not ignoring the difficulties of such attempts at intervention. After all, women's speech was associated with abandon and excess: women are, as Richards and Thorne discuss, included in rhetorical manuals 'not as practitioners of this art, but through their long-standing association with "unruly tropes", and other linguistic "abuses" as analogously disruptive "figures" needing to be brought under control' (2007: 5). To be at once outspoken and silenced is a paradox of power associated with prophetic women far more widely. As Phyllis Mack has argued in her landmark work on visionary women in the seventeenth century, 'the ground of women's authority as spiritual leaders was their achievement of complete self-transcendence' (1992: 5). To be taken seriously, the visionary woman must speak on behalf of external, higher powers, not on her own terms. She is a conduit through which political thought is passed to men, not a political player in her own right: her visions are then both a source of power and shield from criticism, the opportunity to speak and at the same time even more suspect than more usual forms of female public political intervention.

An additional difficulty facing women who would be believed is the association of visions not with the kind of divine authority I have just suggested but – where visions are accepted at all as more than a mere dream – with mental illness. Early modern women who claimed to see visions were more often diagnosed than acknowledged. Katherine Hodgkin finds a connection – even at times a synonymity – between 'witch', 'female prophet', and 'mad woman', and argues that 'because the cultural constraints on appropriate behaviour for women are much more insistent on containment (emotional and physical), excessive or excitable behaviour in women is too easily attributable to mental disorder' (2000: 219). The persistent denigration of female experience as symptomatic of mental illness has, of course, been a significant part of the discourse of feminist criticism over the past fifty years (as, for example, in Sandra M. Gilbert and Susan Gubar's discussion of the binary created between 'angel-women' and 'monster-women' (1979: 44), one which plays out quite literally in the visions of Joan and Katherine, discussed in Section 4. Visions and dreams were believed to result from the failures of the female body, the inability of women to tell the difference between what they 'think they see' and what they do not. As Thibaut Maus de Rolley has noted of demonic visitations, 'the female body was considered to be more porous and open than the male body, and thus more easily invaded and possessed' (2016: 74). Women's bodies were imbalanced; their minds were rapt by imaginary sights; and their testimony was therefore held in doubt. Robert Burton, for instance, ties the false apparitions of the mind to bodily illness: 'If thy heart, brain, liver, spleen be misaffected . . . many diseases accompany, as Incubus, Apoplexy, Epilepsy,

Vertigo, those frequent wakings and terrible dreams . . . they think they see, hear, smell, and touch, that which they do not' (1621: 232).

Dreams are conflated with symptoms which accompany disease: apoplexy, epilepsy, vertigo are all dream experiences for Burton, affecting the senses as much as the dream state itself to create an illness of unreality. Strikingly, this list also contains the state of incubus, or nightmare, thought to stem from possession by or sexual experience with a devil. To dream, to be ill, to be possessed: these states are so similar that Burton can group them without bothering with distinction. Many of the visions discussed here are framed by the men who hear them as madness rather than ecstatic experience. I have no desire to combat this by attempts to diagnose or differentiate between imagination and hallucination, dream and vision. Nor is such a distinction straightforward even within psychiatry: 'Based on epistemic and psychological considerations, the prospect of arriving at a principled way to distinguish delusional from non-delusional beliefs is not promising' (Bortolotti, Gunn, and Sullivan-Bissett, 2016: 48). Rather than categorise each experience (an act which carries inherent judgement about what another's mind finds 'real'), I use 'vision' capaciously, not least because 'visionary' carries a contemporary association of forward thinking as well as future gazing.

Shakespeare's plays show that unruly women who speak disruptively are ultimately brought under control. They are removed from the plot, through absence, active banishment by those onstage, or death. Their political speech is met with disdain at best and often with punishment. If their visions are not wanted, women are easily dismissed as 'mad' and 'misaffected' or else accused of witchcraft. Such misogyny is not confined to history. I want to argue not that Shakespeare's scenes of visionary experience can speak to our own time, but that they must. The vision, as I will argue, is interpreted by its hearers to make its abstract messages comprehensible to the present. Visions then, quite accidentally, offer a model for presentist criticism, a term I use without the disdain with which it has sometimes been associated. This kind of reading looks forwards and backwards and insists that scenes of visionary women do not only speak to a specific historic misogyny, but can be used, as a dream is read, to confront the present and future.

1.2 Conclusion: Seek Further

For Thomas Hill, in his 1576 tract on visionary experience, the interpretation of dreams is a moral imperative. The first example of a prophetic dream in his long treatise is Hecuba's dream of delivering a firebrand instead of a baby: 'It seemeth a thing against nature, and a thing most strange for a woman to be delivered of a firebrand: if Hecuba had left here, and sought no further, then had she not known how her son Paris with whom she then went, should be the destruction of his own country Troy' (Hill, 1576: A7 r). Hecuba seizes the opportunity offered by a dream, which is to read it. The alternative is spelled out: if the dream were dismissed as meaningless, if Hecuba had 'sought no further', then she would not have known that Paris would bring about the destruction of Troy. Yet, the example ends here, and Hill fails to acknowledge the powerlessness and lack of agency that visionary women can face. Hecuba knows what Paris will bring about and is still unable to stop it; if she does tell others about her vision or attempt to react to its warning, Hill makes no mention of it. To have a vision is not to become mistress of fate: it is simply to become witness to it. The vision is a portent that is not necessarily a catalyst for change; visionaries are, like playgoers, compelled to watch, not act.

Nonetheless, the characters discussed in these pages do 'seek further', as Hill would have it, attempting not only to understand their visions but to incite action based on them. Speaking onstage, women claim some control over their own visions. Whereas Hill describes Hecuba's dream and controls his reader's expectations with the warning that it is 'a thing most strange', Shakespeare's visionary women usually describe their own visions. Scenes of women attesting to visions publicly, onstage, are again and again offered as a testing ground on which to examine and often disavow the inherent truthfulness of female testimony. It is rarely that those listening onstage do not believe women have had visions or dreams: it is that those visions are not considered to have any import, and certainly are not important enough to change their hearer's minds. This is then an examination of the control that women attempt to take over the not quite tangible and the not quite real, speaking 'dark matter' aloud without the hope of offering proof.

2 The Art of Dissuasion

Cassandra, a Trojan princess in *Troilus and Cressida*, and Calphurnia, wife of Julius Caesar, have in common their visions of doom and their attempts to dissuade the men close to them from unwise action. Cassandra warns her brother Hector that continuing to fight for Troy is useless: Troy will fall. Calphurnia dreams of her husband bleeding and begs him to avoid the senate on the Ides of March. Neither is successful in this intercession. Peripheral characters within their plays, both women enter the stage only for moments, offer a precise if abstract prophecy of death, and are dismissed not only from the conversation but ultimately from the stage. Both plays prove their visions correct, as Cassandra's brother Hector and Julius Caesar meet their predicted fates, but neither visionary woman is present as a witness to these violent ends and their reactions remain unstaged. These visionaries then exist at a point of possibility, a temporal pivot in which the outcome seems as though it could be changed. Both, however, also exist within a plot that has already been written: the outcome of the Trojan War is stamped in epic poetry, and the death of Caesar is recorded history. These visionaries then have two impossible tasks. Firstly, they must dissuade their brother or husband from a course of action tied to his sense of honour, seeking to stop his ambition rather than to stoke it. Secondly, they must push against the inevitable tide of a narrative that is already surging forward. Looking at these visionaries at once within their present dramatic moment and, as if through double vision, with the metatheatrical awareness of how their story will end, audiences know their persuasive attempts must fail even as their prophecies prove true.

While the classical worlds of Troy and Rome, much like Shakespeare's own, allowed for the possibility of prophecy (and, indeed, sanctioned augury and divination as religious practices), Shakespeare does not present these cultures as ones in which unwavering belief or so-called pagan superstition can be assumed. Despite the fact that one of the three sooth-sayers in Shakespeare is found in *Julius Caesar*, Calphurnia is not granted any prophetic authority (and, crucially, neither is the male soothsayer who warns Caesar of the Ides of March).[6] Despite Cassandra's historical role as

---

[6] The others are found in *Antony and Cleopatra* and *Cymbeline*.

a priestess of Apollo, she is granted no official prophetic role in *Troilus and Cressida*: her title is never mentioned, and she is considered mad, not inspired. What distinguishes Cassandra and Calphurnia from other visionaries is not, then, their historically and geographically remote worlds. They are unlike other female visionaries in Shakespeare because they aim to halt, to dissuade. Cassandra and Calphurnia are anxious playgoers observing their own worlds, running in from the peripheries to try to stop a show that their fellow audience members know must end in blood.

2.1 Cassandra: Raptured Speech

Cassandra's curse is to know the future and not to be believed. Her inability to persuade her father and brother that they will lose the war is tied not only to her apparently loose language – uncontrolled, ineloquent, even mad – but to the ways in which she is made peripheral to the male-led martial debate throughout the play. Her role (like Calphurnia's, discussed in the following) is defined by absence: she appears briefly in Acts 2 and 5 but is otherwise excluded from the plot. Cassandra is contained within and can only burst on stage for brief moments, much like a thought which bubbles to the surface of consciousness only to be repressed. Unable to be heard in her own right, Cassandra calls on those 'Virgins and boys, mid-age, and wrinkled old' who must 'Add to my clamours' (103–5). This appeal for a critical 'mass of moan' (106) only makes the isolation in which Cassandra speaks starker: she appeals to a communal noise that might dissuade the men around her from going out to battle because the strength of her own voice is not enough. Her opening lines demand a choral response which never comes: 'Cry, Trojans, cry!' (2.2.96), 'Lend me ten thousand eyes / And I will fill them with prophetic tears' (100). Cassandra's task, to drive the Trojans to prophetic grief with a contagious, affective sorrow, is not achieved; although she slowly acquires support, it is never enough to turn the tide and dissuade Hector from fighting, even though in their initial encounter he appears moved with 'touches of remorse' (2.2.114) as a result of her 'divination' (113). It is not then that Hector cannot be moved by Cassandra; it is rather that he cannot be moved enough to override his own decisions and instincts. Even this vague sympathy is more than Cassandra usually receives; she is, to Troilus, simply 'our mad sister' (2.2.97).

Because audiences see nothing of Cassandra beyond her brief bursts into the royal family forum, they have no capacity to test the veracity of her claims. There is no explanation as to the mechanics of her visions; they are described simply as 'brainsick raptures' (2.2.121). Rapt by knowledge of the future, Cassandra hurtles forwards, transgressing the gendered rules of conversation by speaking up. Raptures are, elsewhere in Shakespeare, states of unbridled verbal excess, both feminine and infantile, as in *Coriolanus*, when a 'prattling nurse' is imagined to be so distracted as she gossips that she allows the baby in her care to cry itself 'into a rapture' (2.1.203–4).[7] Elsewhere in *Troilus*, Cressida uses the association between female speech and heady rapture to her advantage, both admitting her desire for Troilus and delicately excusing her apparently forward speech by placing the onus for ensuring female silence on him.

> And yet, good faith, I wished myself a man,
> Or that we women had men's privilege
> Of speaking first. Sweet, bid me hold my tongue,
> For in this rapture I shall surely speak
> The thing I shall repent. (3.2.124–8)

The state of rapture implies a lack of agency, an inability to control the truth which flows forth; for Marguerite A. Tassi, 'Raptness is a trance-like experience of deep absorption and fascination, … a violent sensation of being swept away' (2018: 9). Yet, for all of its implications of incontinence, the claim of speaking raptured truth also suggests the kind of useful self-transcendence that Phyllis Mack associates with female prophets, as I discussed earlier. The raptured woman cannot control herself – is not, in fact, entirely herself – and therefore

---

[7] The word 'rapt' is also associated with Macbeth, who is described or describes himself as 'rapt' three times in the play's first act, in response to the vision of the witches (1.3.55, 1.3.141, 1.5.5).

cannot be held accountable for her words. While it suggests the kind of hysterical speech which can be dismissed, an accusation of rapture then also offers women license to break the 'men's privilege / Of speaking first.'

There is a sense too that Cassandra is structurally 'rapt', swept away and propelled on and off stage by the force of her own speeches, unable to be contained by either the play's romantic or martial subplots. In Act 2, Cassandra enters as Troilus's speech is drawn together with a couplet and exits on a closing couplet of her own. Since Shakespeare often uses couplets to mark the end of a scene, Cassandra's bookended interlude appears embedded in a longer scene which is utterly unconcerned with her opinion. Her so-called noise rises between the space of two paired, harmonious rhymes, both concerned with Helen (disgrace/place, woe/go). If rhyme binds concepts together through both sonic and semantic likeness (Rush, 2021: 7), then Cassandra becomes a kind of disruptive free verse in the midst of the monotonous couplets her dialogue defined by staccato repetitions, half-lines, and caesurae. In the face of a hostile audience of men, Cassandra's capacity to express herself is shattered. If *Troilus and Cressida* is, as Gretchen E. Minton has put it, a play '*about* performance anxiety of various kinds – from the basic sexual fear to the most metatheatrical awareness', then Cassandra is surely its most anxious actor, shouting her lines in desperation to a disinterested lords' gallery (2018: 102). In a play made up of anxious, unresolved scenes, Cassandra is not the exception in speaking truth to unheeding ears. She is an emblem of broken communication in a play in which all are cursed not to be heard.

Despite this doubt, Cassandra's prophecy is clear: 'Troy must not be, nor goodly Ilium stand' (2.2.108). Her refrain, 'Cry, Trojans, cry!', repeated six times in the mere thirteen lines she speaks in Act 2, offers insistent doom without extraneous details. Her hints of what will come are powerfully simple, requiring no exposition. In a play made up of repetitive and self-contradictory speeches between politicians on both sides, Cassandra's plain warnings are arresting. Yet, despite this clarity, Cassandra is coded 'mad', entering 'with her hair about her ears' (2.2.99, s.d.), a representation which is, as David Bevington observes, echoed in Thomas Heywood's *The Iron Age, Part 1* (c. 1612–13) (1998: 429). Still, in *1 Iron Age*, Cassandra is at least acknowledged in the dramatis personae as 'a Prophetess' (Heywood, 1632: A2v). Moreover, Heywood's Trojans are less casually cruel than Shakespeare's. In Heywood, Paris acknowledges his sister with 'What intends Cassandra?' (B2r), creating space for her response even if that response is immediately undercut by Priam's decisive line, 'Cassandra's mad'. Even then, Cassandra argues back: 'You are mad, all Troy is mad'. Moreover, Heywood's Hector defends his sister as a 'Vestal Prophetess' (B2v), unlike Shakespeare's Hector who speaks only three words directly to his sister: 'Peace, sister, peace!' (2.2.103). Only after Cassandra's exit does Shakespeare's Hector appear sympathetic, as discussed earlier, describing her 'high strains / Of divination' (2.2.112–13) and attributing to the disbelieving Troilus the 'madly hot' (115) blood that Troilus himself attributes to Cassandra. In understanding Cassandra's speech as a sign of bodily imbalance, however, Heywood's and Shakespeare's Trojans agree. Madly hot blood suggests that visions are symptoms of illness in a body not raptured by divine inspiration but ravaged by disease.

Despite her isolated and apparently imbalanced speech in Act 2, Cassandra at last gains the ally for whom she has been pleading. Hector's wife, Andromache, has also had dreams which 'will sure prove ominous to the day' (5.3.6), although Hector dismisses these in a mere half-line. By Act 5, however, the Hector who felt a twinge of remorse is now fixed on his course, too far into the war to stop now. The two women work together, kneeling to Hector (as Calphurnia kneels to Caesar), 'consor[ting]' in 'loud and dear petition' (5.3.9). For a brief moment, two peripheral women, both of whom know through visions that Hector will die in battle, find strength in their shared experience. In this moment of solidarity, Shakespeare (as so often in the play) deviates from the *Iliad*.[8] In Book 6, Andromache does beseech Hector not to fight, but not because of a dream. Moreover, this intervention is not only far earlier in the narrative of Hector's fall, given Hector's death in Book 22, but is also spoken by Andromache alone. By bringing both women onstage to speak

---

[8] Of course, the *Iliad* was not Shakespeare's only source: as Bevington notes, Shakespeare may also have been drawing on a range of contemporary but now lost plays on the Trojan War (1998: 409–10).

in consort and by attributing a dream of 'bloody turbulence' (5.3.11) to Andromache, making her a secondary visionary, Shakespeare doubles the strength of their warning, rendering Hector twice as foolish for dismissing both his wife and his sister. Two women's voices are not enough.

By Cassandra's third and final appearance, later in the same scene, she has gained a more powerful supporter still: her father, King Priam. Now Priam is convinced, not by Cassandra alone but by the weight of evidence which includes his own prophetic experience:

> Thy wife hath dreamt, thy mother hath had visions,
> Cassandra doth foresee, and I myself
> Am like a prophet suddenly *enrapt*
> To tell thee that this day is ominous. (5.3.65–8, my emphasis)

Troy is suddenly full of visionaries, and Priam, who appeared ambivalent to his daughter's prophecies, now shares them, or at least aligns himself with them through simile.[9] But even with all the patriarchal authority offered by Priam, Hector will not listen. Cassandra has already hinted that prophecy might be a communal experience, one shared by the collective conscious-ness of a nation under siege. In her first appearance, she invokes the shared moans of fellow Trojans of all ages and genders; now, her own prophetic power is catching, as it spreads to Andromache, Hecuba, and Priam, who plead with Hector to break his oath and refuse to fight. Priam's final, fractious conversation with Hector ends with the two exiting 'severally' (97, s.d.), an emblem of disunity that underscores a sharp farewell. The separate exits suggest that prophecies fracture the harmony between men (or rather between political groups of men), fulfilling the (similarly unheeded) warning that Ulysses offers in Act 1: 'What plagues and what portents ... / ... rend and deracinate / The unity and married calm of states' (1.3.96–100). Cassandra contains within herself a microcosm of this

---

[9] To this list, Fly adds both Thersites and Achilles, whose prediction of Hector's death – one drawn from intuition rather than from visionary experience – he calls 'clairvoyant knowledge' (1975: 158).

discord, giving flesh to fears which the Trojans will not voice and offering them truth which they cannot accept without pedantic debate.

Even after Priam attests to his own vision, or perhaps claims to have been rapt by the women around him as if by prophecy, the women onstage are blamed for the folly of claiming to see the future. Troilus dismisses the warning with an insult that might be addressed to either Andromache, who has just been made to exit, or Cassandra, who remains, but which does not criticise Priam: 'This foolish, dreaming, superstitious girl / Makes all these bodements' (5.3.82–3). Yet, Troilus does not have the last word. Cassandra finishes his line of pentameter with the resolution, 'O, farewell. dear Hector!' (83). In these final lines, Cassandra ignores Troilus and turns the question of sight back onto her brother, Hector, directing his gaze: 'Look how thou diest; look how thy eye turns pale' (84). Cassandra calls upon visionary sight which Hector does not share and asks him to see the two things which cannot be seen: one's own death, and one's own eye. For Hector, prophetic sight is impossible even when he is told where to look. Cassandra has prophesised; 'Hecuba cries out' (86); Andromache 'shrills her dolours forth' (87) but none of these 'witless antics' (89), as the visionaries seem, are taken seriously. Even Priam is dismissed: Hector bends his knee to ask for permission to fight but does not wait for an answer. Visionary experience is so thoroughly dismissed as madness that even King Priam's intervention makes little difference.

Ending with the death of Hector, at once utterly expected and deeply shocking, the play judges Cassandra's visions and finds them true, but it does not decide whether those visons are divinely sent, or just the good guesses or even the reasonable paranoia of a woman living through siege warfare. Her visions spread throughout her family, to Andromache, Hecuba, and Priam, but these shared moments of testimony are treated as if they were a shared psychosis, spread amongst a family in a moment of trauma. Of Cassandra's own fate, the play says nothing: by omitting any sense of her personal narrative, it contains her only within three fragmented vignettes, unable to exist beyond the moments she wrests from a play far more sympathetic to violence than to visions.

2.2 Calphurnia: Second-hand Dreams

If *Julius Caesar* is a tragedy of two parts, with the death of Caesar at its centre, then Calphurnia is found only 'before'. Where Cassandra punctuates *Troilus and Cressida*, drawing focus back to inevitable doom until the final act, Calphurnia falls out of her play entirely. Her agency in *Julius Caesar*, such as it is, centres around her prophetic dream of Caesar's death. After his death, both the dream and Calphurnia appear to have served their purpose and disappear. Moreover, in the two scenes in which she appears onstage, Calphurnia moves only according to Caesar's design. She is called onstage by Caesar, told where to stand ('directly in Antonio's way' (1.2.5)), and exits with Caesar moments later. Beyond establishing her existence, Calphurnia's presence in her first scene is hardly necessary at all. She does not react when Caesar warns Antony to touch his wife during the fertility ritual of the Lupercalia, nor when Brutus observes her pallor. In the brief moments she spends onstage, however, Calphurnia does stand as a wordless witness to an interaction between Caesar and a soothsayer who delivers the fatal line: 'Beware the ides of March' (1.2.25). Although they share a significant fate – neither is believed – the soothsayer is established as Calphurnia's prophetic foil: he cries out for Caesar's attention while she stands in silence and pushes through the crowd while she is carefully positioned. He also speaks his own prophecy, whereas Calphurnia, as I will discuss, does not. Through her silent presence, Calphurnia is at once aligned with soothsaying and positioned only at its periphery, as she is at the periphery of the play.

Calphurnia then enters the stage for the second and final time to hear her own dream recounted onstage by Caesar: she endures the dissonance of not only seeing the dream of her husband's body as statue, bleeding from multiple wounds, but now of hearing the living Caesar describe it. In Plutarch, as translated by Thomas North, Caesar is the spectator who watches Calphurnia 'weep and sigh, and put forth many fumbling lamentable speeches' in her sleep (1579: 793). Instead, Shakespeare gives Caesar the role of describing the dream (or rather, of recounting Calphurnia's sleeping words onstage). By speaking it himself, Caesar wrests control of the dream from Calphurnia, with his onstage echo of his wife's words 'suggesting that female wisdom is always already appropriated by men, the better to be disposed of' (Roulon, 2016:

136). Calphurnia's vision becomes a passive experience, reframed solely for its effect on Caesar. Despite Plutarch's emphasis on the imprecision of her 'fumbling' words, Shakespeare's Caesar describes a far sharper account of his wife's dream: 'Thrice hath Calphurnia in her sleep cried out / "Help, ho! They murder Caesar!"' (2.2.2–3). This clarity makes Caesar's final refusal to listen to the dream appear absurdly reckless: this is not a mumble, but a statement, repeated three times as rhetorical emphasis demands. This sense of certainty is tempered in Plutarch by the admission that other sources (Livy) suggest that the dream was of a torn gable rather than Caesar's body. Shakespeare offers no ambiguity, despite the scene's continual drive towards doubt: there is one clear dream, and Caesar dismisses it.

As the scene progresses, Calphurnia tries to wrest back agency over the dream, despite knowing her word is not enough. This is not the moment of rapture that sweeps Cassandra in a state of seeming madness; it is a calm, planned intervention from a politician's wife. Yet, before she enters or speaks, Caesar has already sent out word to the patriarchal and religious structures which make up the power of Rome, asking for their opinions. Only once this call for alternative augury has been sought is Calphurnia finally seen and heard, despite the fact that in Plutarch, Calphurnia is the one who urges Caesar to seek other proofs if he will not accept the truth of her vision. Instead of turning to priests, Shakespeare has Calphurnia invoke the shared visions of other citizens, recounted second-hand as Caesar recounted her own dream second-hand. Repeating the vision of the soldiers of the watch, she describes a meteorological omen, in which

> Fierce fiery warriors fight upon the clouds,
> In ranks and squadrons and right form of war,
> Which drizzled blood upon the Capitol.
> The noise of battle hurtled in the air.
> Horses do neigh, and dying men did groan,
> And ghosts did shriek and squeal about the streets. (2.2.19–24)

It is difficult to tell whether, in the one moment of extended speech she is granted, Calphurnia's description of a shared vision that she herself did not share has slipped into metaphor: the vision of warring soldiers in the clouds echoes a passage from Nashe's *The Terrors of the Night* (1594) in which Nashe describes visions which emerge from the fumes of melancholy: 'whole armies of men skirmishing in the air, dragons, wild beasts, bloody streamers, blazing comets, fiery streaks with other apparitions innumerable'. In *Terrors*, published five years before *Julius Caesar* was first performed, airy soldiers are the product of a vaporous mind: any playgoer recalling Nashe would associate the vision that Calphurnia describes with bodily imbalance. Indeed, even for the brief time that he is swayed by Calphurnia, Caesar cannot resist alluding to the supposed fragility of the female body. Sleeplessness and its resultant hallucinations were associated with an imbalance of the humours (Fretz, 2016: 5–8). When Caesar does agree to stay away from the forum, it is therefore with a weighted concession: 'And for thy humour I will stay at home' (2.2.56). Here humour is both inclination and, more literally, bodily fluid: Caesar is not moved (or will not acknowledge being moved) by the vision, but by the humour which has created a false image in his wife's mind. The vision is tolerated as a sign of mental weakness (and as a useful excuse for Caesar, who is equivocating about a journey to the senate which is so freighted with ill omens).

Her dream alone is not enough, and Calphurnia's invocation of a group of witnesses (and one witness's particular description of armies in the clouds) only weakens her case. Caesar believes that if visions are widespread, their prophetic power is cheapened or diluted, as if their power lies in their exclusivity and the personal advantage that exclusive knowledge might offer: 'Yet Caesar shall go forth, for these predictions / Are to the world in general as to Caesar' (2.2.28–9). Caesar's wilful refusal to heed his wife's warning is, moreover, typical of his refusal to consider the warnings of Artemidorus and the soothsayer (Schupak, 2016: 125).[10] For Caesar, the only second opinions that he values when deciding on the veracity of prophecies come from men of rank. Following Caesar's decision to avoid the forum, Decius Brutus enters the scene to offer

---

[10] This name recalls the dream theorist Artemidorus whose work, already translated from Greek into Latin and French, was published in English in 1606 as *The Judgement, or Exposition of Dreams*. For Caesar to ignore a warning from such a character suggests his wilful refusal to listen.

a persuasive reframing of Calphurnia's dream. Decius Brutus's ability to turn the interpretation of the dream on its head and argue that the blood running from the statue of Caesar is the lifeblood of Rome itself suggests the malleability of oneiromancy (dream reading). Shakespeare follows Plutarch in invoking Caesar's toxic insecurities, framing the idea of returning to the senate only 'when Calpurnia should have better dreams' (North, 1579: 793) not only in terms of superstition but of fragile male pride. The vision is not enough to dissuade Caesar in the face of a greater threat: the laughter of other men.

In a world full of accepted prophecies (Decius Brutus does not deny Calphurnia's dream but rather its interpretation), Calphurnia is dismissed, despite the fact that her dream – unlike Casca's and Cassius's which are heard elsewhere – is sharp and precise. In its accuracy it is rivalled only by the Soothsayer's prophecy which warns of a particular day, not of a particular event. Even then, the Soothsayer's fleeting encounter with Portia, as both hurry through the streets of Rome, reveals that his prophecy is not certain: 'None that I know will be, / Much that I fear may chance' (2.4.32–3). Calphurnia's dream is the moment at which Caesar's death is first played out and at which its inevitability is sealed. Brief as it is, Calphurnia's dream is the centre of the play, around which the temporal axes of foreknowledge and retrospection pivot. Yet, the moment which seems to stage the possibility that Caesar might change his mind offers only false hope. The play even predicts Calphurnia's failed prediction. In the scene before her dream takes place, the disbelief with which it will be heard has already been decided. Cassius worries that Caesar has become credulous of 'apparent prodigies, / The unaccustomed terror of this night' (2.1.198–9) – it is hard not to hear Nashe's title, *The Terrors of the Night*, in this line – and sends Decius to 'o'ersway' him (203). Even before Calphurnia has shared her dream, it is fated to be misinterpreted: she cannot stop Caesar.

2.3 Conclusion

The visions of Cassandra and Calphurnia offer only the illusion of change. Both women speak against the tide of fate and the momentum of the tragic narrative within which they exist. Cassandra is cursed never to be believed;

Calphurnia may win her husband round for a moment, but ultimately cannot dissuade him when pitted against the driving forces of his own pride and his apparent destiny. Following the model of Pilate's wife's dream, discussed earlier, these vision scenes not only reveal the failure of female political interventions, even within the firmly domestic role of concerned wife or sister, but also allow for the staging of political men as unwise listeners. Hector and Caesar emerge from these vision scenes as reckless husbands and rash politicians. Both men are temporarily, if not swayed, then sympathetic to the prophecies they hear, but neither will commit to a course of action based on the words of a woman. In fact, the consequences of not listening to Cassandra and Calphurnia take up far more stage time than either can claim herself.

Cassandra and Calphurnia both warn of impending death, and in doing so both speak directly to the man whose death is foreseen. Both have some success. Cassandra articulates her visions and in the course of the play acquires more support, although she is never able to dissuade her brother Hector from his course of further fighting. Calphurnia is briefly able to dissuade Caesar from attending the senate meeting at which he will be killed. Ultimately, however, the power of visionary experience is wrested from both: Cassandra needs not only her sister-in-law Andromache but also her father, the Trojan king Priam, to share her experience in order to gain any traction with her brother, and Calphurnia's dream is only given attention when it is recited by Caesar and interpreted by Decius Brutus. As such, both women become peripheral to their own visions, unable to claim ownership over their own cognitive experiences. The vision becomes, when convenient, the product of the unbalanced female body, rapt with emotion: the power of diagnosis lies with men who are predisposed to dismiss the vision as a symptom, not an experience. The vision can be taken from their hands and parsed for political ends when what Calphurnia and Cassandra want is simply *an* end, *the* end, a scene cut mercifully short.

3 Ambitious Visions and/as Sinful Thought

Both Eleanor, Duchess of Gloucester, and Lady Macbeth understand the role prophecy might play in political advancement. Drawing the two women together, Alison Findlay has suggested that 'The damaging effects explored through Eleanor's role provide a prototype for the role of Lady Macbeth' (2010: 123). Certainly, Eleanor's willingness to pay for Jordan's necromancy to further her ends is echoed in Lady Macbeth's use of the witches' visions as far as they suit her purposes. Both women are drawn to the political power of prophecies, the way that future-gazing can itself influence the future. Yet, while both women begin their plays with ambitious dreams, those dreams ultimately falter. Whereas Eleanor is arrested and banished, Lady Macbeth is utterly destroyed by haunting visions of the past. These women, overtly political, clever, and engaged, experience dreams which are suggested to be the result of their own damaged psyches, not of divine (or even demonic) inspiration. Lady Macbeth's somnam-bulant visions of her bloody hands, caught between the states of waking and sleeping, are suggestive of an obsessive return to memory; Eleanor makes no secret that she is continually thinking of the ambitious climb which shapes her own dream of her coronation at Westminster. Yet, this turn to interiority does not simply serve to examine the rich and often troubled inner lives of two female characters: it also serves to suggest that their prophetic dreams are the result of their own sin, not of some higher knowledge. The dreams discussed in this section are associated with delirium, madness, and, most troublingly of all, with witchcraft. In *2 Henry VI* and *Macbeth*, dreams of politics and ambition emerge as a space in which women might be corrupted (or, like witches, might corrupt).

In early modern culture, the vision could be understood as a revelation of the secret self rather than a moment of access to a higher truth; the inter-pretation of visions could be framed as an act of introspection. In an essay on dreams, written c. 1650, Thomas Browne dismisses any possibility that dreams offer true visions. Dreams could, however, offer insight into the self: 'Men act in sleep with some conformity unto their awaked senses; and consolations or discouragements may be drawn from dreams which inti-mately tell us ourselves' (1991: 19). The use of dreams, Browne claims, is not to look outwards towards unknown futures, but to better understand one's own interior and present self. Both Eleanor and Lady Macbeth experience dreams or hallucinations which seem indicative of their apparent failures of thought: their ambition, their jealousy, their guilt. And, as if to confirm that their visions are self-induced signs of sin, both Eleanor and Lady Macbeth are punished for seeking to manifest their dreams of power, Eleanor with a public shaming, Lady Macbeth with private trauma. The warning is clear: women who not only imagine but actively seek a more powerful future will be curtailed. Having attempted with differing success to place their husbands in the position of king, both women are removed from the narrative. By sharing their dreams, these women show their hands, and must pay for it.

3.1 Eleanor of Gloucester: Presumptuous Sight

2 Henry VI begins with two opposing exchanges between husbands and wives. The first scene sees King Henry VI greet his new bride Margaret of Anjou (a visionary woman discussed further in Section 5) with public fanfare; the second reveals Humphrey and Eleanor, the Duke and Duchess of Gloucester, sharing their dreams in private. This scene begins with Eleanor's attempt to redirect her husband's gaze in a negotiation of sight and perspective, in the first of the scene's several extended uses of the imagery of rising and falling:

> Why are thine eyes fixed to the sullen earth,
> Gazing on that which seems to dim thy sight?
> What seest thou there? King Henry's diadem
> Enchased with all the honours of the world?
> If so, gaze on, and grovel on thy face
> Until thy head be circled with the same. (1.2.5–10)

Gloucester's line of sight and, therefore, his ambitions are too lowly for Eleanor and therefore she tells him where to look. She imposes meaning upon his bowed head, suggesting symbolism where none exists and introducing the suggestion of a crown: she reads the scene in front of her as if it were a dream, full of meaningful messages, to which she can add messages of her own.

> We'll both together lift our heads to heaven
> And never more abase our sight so low
> As to vouchsafe one glance unto the ground. (1.2.11–16)

In a rhetorical feat, Eleanor argues that Gloucester should raise his sight from the ground, where he sees the crown, to heaven, where he will still see the crown. Eleanor's manipulation of Gloucester's gaze suggests the psychological suppression known as ironic process theory, in which the more the thinker struggles to suppress a thought, the harder it is to think of anything else. In other words, whatever Gloucester was thinking of when he lowered his eyes, he is now thinking of the crown. Eleanor is not simply visionary; she carefully controls Gloucester's vision, turning his gaze upwards, although her own will soon, given her involvement in necromancy, turn towards the hell space of the playhouse, where power seems to come from below. She turns Gloucester's gaze towards their apparently shared goal, inserting herself in a line of sight that she can guide.

This exchange now turns to actual dreams. Unlike the scenes I have discussed so far in which women are the primary dreamers here Gloucester first recounts his own dream: his staff of office was broken, and the heads of Somerset and Suffolk were mounted on pieces of the staff. The dream is immediately dismissed by Eleanor not as meaningless (dreams must have meaning in order for her own to matter) but as having a simple 'argument' that she can explain: those who challenge Gloucester will be punished. Yet, interpreting Gloucester's dream is her contingency plan; Eleanor had tried to dismiss his dream entirely. Even before he offers a description of the dream, Eleanor offers to 'requite it / With sweet rehearsal' (23–4) of her own dream – a morning dream, moreover, and therefore widely understood in early modern culture to be true (Knowles, 1999: 167). When the audience finally hear Gloucester's dream, it appears to be unambiguous: the heads of Suffolk and Somerset are placed on Gloucester's own broken staff of state. Shakespeare rarely offers a more explicit dream, predicting the downfall of three men who all die in the course of the play, yet Eleanor, like Decius Brutus when faced with Calphurnia's dream, offers a clearly subjective reading which acknowledges the danger to Suffolk and Somerset but omits the danger to Gloucester. This is not the only way in which the dream scene in *2 Henry VI* offers a model to be inverted a decade later in *Caesar*: where Calphurnia is accused of being 'humorous', Eleanor deems her husband 'choleric' (51) and dismisses his dreams as symptoms of bodily imbalance.

Skating over Gloucester's dream in three lines, Eleanor then distracts from further debate by offering a dream of her own, one in which she sits in Westminster for her coronation. Jean Howard and Phyllis Rackin suggest that Eleanor discloses too much: 'Rushing to recount her own dream, Eleanor inadvertently reveals the role she will play in Gloucester's impending downfall' (1997: 74). That Eleanor articulates her real desires for the future in the deniable guise of a dream suggests that her dream vision is a manifestation of personal ambition played out in abstract form. For Eleanor, a dream's power exists in its potentiality, not in its prophetic truth: it is not a supernatural message but a rhetorical tool. Eleanor is, as Gloucester dismisses her in turn, 'Presumptuous' (42) both in the sense of over-reaching and of over-interpreting. Through this epithet, Eleanor is aligned with the rhetorical figure George Puttenham calls 'the presumptuous', defined as presupposing what an opponent will say in debate: 'we do prevent them of their advantage, and do catch the ball (as they are wont to say) before it come to the ground' (1589: 194).[11] In interrupting Gloucester with a dream of her own, Eleanor successfully employs a rhetorical device which is itself a kind of prognostication, intuiting what her rhetorical opponent (her husband) will argue, and countering it with an equally vivid description. Eleanor's opening speech therefore carefully pre-empts her husband's arguments and manipulates him towards taking ownership of both a prophetic dream and an ambition which belong to Eleanor. That ambition is disguised as fate.

In 1.4, Eleanor's attempt to claim control over prophecy is exerted more literally in her employment of two necromancers. Having paid Margery Jordan, the 'cunning witch' (1.2.75), and Roger Bolingbroke, the 'conjuror' (76), to raise a prophetic spirit, Eleanor enters 'aloft' (1.4.12, s.d.) to watch the results. From her position above the stage, Eleanor takes the god's eye view, and yet is positioned so that she is unequivocally visible: in this moment of seeing and being seen, she might be an emblem of the visionary woman. Her position above also recalls both epic and biblical necromancy, in which a prophetic spirit is drawn up from the ground (such as the *nekyia* through which Odysseus summons the prophet Tiresias in Book XI of the *Odyssey* or the moment when the Witch of Endor raises Samuel from the grave in 1 Samuel). Despite

---

[11] Puttenham associates the presumptuous with women and ascribes to women a propensity for hidden knowledge and for fickleness: '[the presumptuous] is also when we will not seem to know a thing, and yet we know it well enough, and may be likened to the manner of women, who as the common saying is, will say nay and take it' (1589: 194).

Eleanor's earlier dismissal of her husband's downturned gaze, knowledge is drawn up from below; in the playhouse, the spirit rises from the hell space beneath the stage. Although not carrying out the rites, Eleanor is positioned above as the agent of this necromancy, raising the demonic up into the playhouse and into the court.

The spirit (whose name, ASNATH, is a simple anagram for SATHAN) offers prophecies which are both real and riddling: predictions of death which only make sense after the fact. To emphasise this semantic uncertainty, the prophecies are voiced and written multiple times, with each transfer risking a slip or false transcription. The questions for the spirit are written or dictated by Eleanor, then read aloud by Bolingbroke; the answers are then spoken by the spirit, and in turn written down by Bolingbroke or Southwell; they are then read aloud by York as evidence of Eleanor's treason, who adds his own commentary as he reads. This circulation of prophetic information from paper to voice obscures Eleanor's agency.[12] Despite paying for this necromancy, and gazing on all from above, Eleanor only hears the spirit's words while the men below her read, write, and recount them. Margery's role is similarly curtailed. While Margery appears to begin the interrogation, it is Bolingbroke who immediately steps in to ask the questions; following this, Margery does not speak again. Margery 'lies down upon her face' (1.4.12, s.d.) and whispers to the devils, taking the same lowly position which Eleanor describes with scorn when insulting Gloucester: 'grovel on thy face'. Both women are carefully positioned: lying on the stage establishes Margery as Eleanor's foil, engaged in the necromancy and yet barely visible to audiences standing level with the stage. Gloucester's words prove prescient, as Eleanor now looks from the 'top of honour to disgrace's feet', her ambition proved, as Gloucester warned, to be 'treachery'.

---

[12] Levine suggests that Eleanor's narrative agency is wrested from her by Buckingham, who enters the stage to share news of her arrest: 'As it inscribes the duchess's treason within the familiar narrative of virago-witch-traitor, Buckingham's report gains a certain authority, for the characters onstage and perhaps for some members of Shakespeare's London audience' (1994: 104). This retrospective retelling of a woman's visionary experience also prefigures Caesar's retelling of Calphurnia's dream (discussed in Section 2).

For all Eleanor's apparent financial and rhetorical mastery over prophecy, however, she too is victim to manipulation. She has been induced to seek out the prophetic powers of the spirit by Hume, who has been hired by Suffolk and Cardinal Beaufort to 'buzz these conjurations in her brain' (1.2.99). This fall is facilitated by Queen Margaret, who complains about Eleanor's ambition to Suffolk and who is examined as a visionary woman in Section 5, primarily in her iteration in *Richard III*. This art of suggestion works on Eleanor, just as it worked for her in her conversation with Gloucester, and she is soon arrested for her part in the necromancy. Her final humiliation both invokes and revokes the powerful role she has played in the opening act of the play. As she is led barefoot through the streets, Eleanor once again becomes the object of the audience's sight, although not now because of her prominent position above. Her warning to Gloucester, 'Look how they gaze' (2.4.21) both engulfs Gloucester within Eleanor's embarrassment – he too is being watched – and implicates the audience in this ritual of looking, making any spectator culpable simply because they are watching the play itself. The paper trail of Asnath's words described earlier is now recalled as verses pinned to Eleanor's back, the prophecies replaced by slander. Eleanor's capacity to look ahead (to think 'presumptuously') turns towards a prediction of how she will remember this day when Gloucester merely 'stood by' (2.4.46). Finally seeing her future as a fall, not a rise, Eleanor understands her fate not through visionary inspiration but through political instinct.

For Eleanor, prophecies are tools to be fabricated and bought. In a brief, eight-line soliloquy, Eleanor reveals that her relationship to prophecy and to political culture is not passive: 'being a woman, I will not be slack / To play my part in fortune's pageant' (1.2.66–7). Fortune, or fate, or the future, is a performance, and one in which Eleanor will play an intelligent and auton-omous role. Yet, Eleanor's influence ends sharply with Act 2. Knowledge of the future once seemed a shrewd investment, but the price Eleanor pays is not only a ritual humiliation which excludes her from the court but a removal from the play itself. The memory of her actions, however – and in particular her capacity to buy visionary influence through the necromantic powers of others – taints the rest of the play's prophetic proclamations, not least as the deaths predicted by the spirit do in fact take place. Eleanor's influence lingers after her sharp exit: the 'bedlam brainsick Duchess' is still on Suffolk's mind in Act 3

(3.1.51) and the punishment she suffers may remain in a playgoer's memory when the Cardinal admits that he too has seen God's 'secret judgement' in a dream' (3.2.31). She is recalled visually in 4.5, when Lord Scales stands above the revolting citizens below in the same configuration as Eleanor and the conjurers and spirit below, suggesting that his authority is just as suspect. Eleanor dominates the first acts of the play only to be silenced, but, as she makes clear in her brief soliloquy, Eleanor would rather be silenced than never speak at all.

3.2 *Lady Macbeth: Sick Visions*

Following his encounter with the witches, Macbeth seems to catch their capacity for seeing visions. He is the seer of the play, hallucinating daggers and ghosts. For the first four acts of the tragedy, Lady Macbeth's role is not, unlike many of the other visionaries discussed here, to petition her husband because of her visions (although she does petition him on behalf of the witches). Her role is more active: to make manifest what Macbeth sees. Initially, therefore, Lady Macbeth seems only a facilitator of visionary experience. Macbeth's famous 'fatal vision' (2.1.36), the dagger he imagines or hallucinates as he contemplates the murder of Duncan, is made real by Lady Macbeth, who actually does place a dagger before her husband: 'Hark! – I laid their daggers ready; / He could not miss 'em' (2.2.12–13). Whereas Macbeth believes in prophecy and the augury of 'maggot-pies and choughs and rooks' (124), in the first half of the tragedy Lady Macbeth is willing to accept Macbeth's supernatural encounters largely for the political opportunities they offer. Yet, in the final act, all suddenly pivots. As if prophecy is pushing at its seams, *Macbeth* seems unable to contain two visionaries, or two tragic falls. The Macbeths' visionary experiences never overlap. Although Act 4 has seen the witches offer a catalogue of apparitions to Macbeth – an armed head, a bloody child, a crowned child, eight kings, and Banquo – in Act 5, all visions belong to Lady Macbeth. Her troubled sleepwalking, her inner sickness, seems to be inherited from Macbeth. While Tassi distinguishes between Cassandra and Lady Macbeth in claiming that the latter 'infects' those around her with 'the malignant potency of [her] visions', Lady Macbeth seems more infected than infectious: the suggestion of physical and mental illness is present throughout her last scenes.

Lady Macbeth's visionary experience in Act 5 comes as if by sudden illness rather than by demonic influence. Macbeth's visions are created by external forces; Lady Macbeth's are generated within.[13] Macbeth's experiences are highly visualised: from his ekphrasis of the dagger before him to the presence of Banquo onstage, everything Macbeth sees, the audience also sees. Lady Macbeth's visions are starkly internal, invisible to those around her. A fleeting suggestion that Lady Macbeth seeks paranormal influence is her address to the 'spirits / That tend on mortal thoughts' (39–40), but even here the supernatural and cognitive are deeply interwoven. The effect of the spirits, too, is not to offer visions but to influence her body: the spirits are 'murd'ring ministers' (47) that might make toxic her breast milk and allow her body to poison whatever might try to consume it. If the speech is read as an incantation, then it is a failed one: no spirits attend, as they so evidently do elsewhere in Shakespeare at the behest of necromantic women. As tempting as it is to suggest that Lady Macbeth begins the play with a connection to the supernatural world (she seems to echo the witches in referring to the 'all-hail hereafter', 54, but in fact simply echoes her husband's letter), it is vital that Lady Macbeth's actions are not influenced by any supernatural power. She can 'feel now / The future in the instant' (56–7), but because of her own intuition, not because of a demonic vision. Surprisingly, as so many visionaries are treated with suspicion, the hints of visionary experience associated with Lady Macbeth actually serve to mask the less palatable reality of her violent ambition. The sight of bloody hands, accompanied by the 'smell of the blood still' (48), actually suggests a sensory imprint of trauma. Trauma resists forgetting: as Cathy Caruth argues in her theory-defining work, trauma 'is not assimilated fully at the time, but only belatedly, in its repeated possession

---

[13] The exception might be the dagger, which Lesel Dawson argues is the product of 'mental fixation, a cognitive disturbance in which an extremely pleasing or terrifying image is forcefully imprinted on the brain' (2020: 9). The dagger, which both the Macbeths encounter in the murder of Duncan, and which Lady Macbeth seems to hold, psychically, forever, as the blood on her hands suggests, is then a pivotal vision which unites their fixated minds.

of the one who experiences it' (1995: 4). Hallucinations only push Lady Macbeth backwards, inverting the role of the vision which is to offer foresight.

The question of Lady Macbeth's visions is then not what they mean (audiences know well where the imagined blood has come from) but why they are happening. This debate is centred around the Doctor who is brought to observe Lady Macbeth's sleepwalking. The Doctor claims that 'infected minds / To their deaf pillows will discharge their secrets' (69–70) but then appears unsure if her mental infection is medical: 'More needs she the divine than the physician' (71). There is a suggestion that Lady Macbeth's mind is not infected so much as possessed. Resisting the kind of binary between the super-natural and medical that the Doctor proposes, however, Dympna Callaghan cautions that mental illness and witchcraft were often understood and treated in much the same ways: 'the witch in Jacobean culture had become the hysteric, a scientific phenomenon rather than a disturbing threat to phallic power' (1992: 369).[14] Lady Macbeth's interiority, the reality of her mental trauma, is diminished by the Doctor's implication of possession, her actions attributed neither to remorse nor to personal illness but to demonic forces. Just as sleepwalking positions Lady Macbeth between the dream space of sleep and waking awareness, it also positions her between conscious and unconscious thought. Trauma can be a moment caught between performance and recol-lection: 'is the subject's return to the "origin" of the trauma – in flashbacks and nightmares, and so on – a literal re-enactment of the event, or a representation of it?' (Starks-Estes, 2014: 18). Remembering and re-enacting, Lady Macbeth is caught in the trauma of a past scene which is now embellished with her guilt. She is an actress forced to repeat her lines, filling the stage with imagined sensory effects in order to relive a murder. Audiences watch Lady Macbeth remembering a scene that they remember too but are unable to get access to her vision beyond her scattered descriptions and their own imaginings. This distance – this utter uncertainty as to what Lady Macbeth can see – serves to unsettle the play's reality, as Act 5 seems to

[14] For more on the overlapping connections between exorcism, witchcraft, and hysteria, see Levin, who argues that 'The demonic woman and the hysteric violated patriarchal ideals, but they validated misogynist accounts of an essentially corrupted female nature' (2002: 29).

slip from tragedy into abstract morality play. Emma Smith argues that 'often Shakespeare stages that very nothingness behind our interpretations, refusing to give us any access to the event itself, only its subsequent and contested readings' (2019: 151). Lady Macbeth's visions are 'nothingness', neither quite message nor memory, and the attempts of the Doctor and Macbeth to understand them leads to nothingness too.

Because they do not suit his ambitions, as her encouraging use of the witches' prophecies once did, Macbeth treats his wife's hallucinations as illnesses. His first reaction to her 'thick-coming fancies' (5.3.40) is an abrupt half-line: 'Cure her of that' (41). The doctor, who is so roundly unhelpful as to appear parodic, still turns away from medical treatment.

Macbeth   Canst thou not minister to a mind diseased,
            Pluck from the memory a rooted sorrow,
            Raze out the written troubles of the brain,
            And with some sweet oblivious antidote
            Cleanse the fraught bosom of that perilous stuff
            Which weighs upon the heart?
Doctor   Therein the patient
            Must minister to himself. (5.3.41–8)

Macbeth suggests that visionary experience is the result of excess, of emotions that cannot escape the mind but remain festering there. He describes a sorrow that is 'rooted', troubles that are 'written', a weight upon the heart: paradoxically, permanence of thought is associated with an instability in the mind. 'Rooted' also recalls his own first encounter with the witches; Banquo proposes that the encounter might in fact have been a drug-induced hallucination: 'have we eaten on the insane root / That takes the reason prisoner?' (1.3.82–3). Banquo turns more readily to bodily explanations than to the supernatural, despite the fact that the play is dripping with all the markers of the supernatural, from ghosts to omens. Medical or even chemical imbalance may serve as an excuse for Lady Macbeth but this does not generate sympathy. The Doctor's final diagnosis lays the blame on Lady Macbeth: her visions are self-induced and must be self-treated.

The Doctor is, however, emphatically not the authority on Lady Macbeth's visions. The primary witness to Lady Macbeth's sleepwalking is an unnamed gentlewoman, a character who does not appear elsewhere in the play. The gentlewoman understands the visionary state far more clearly than the attendant physician, especially in the following exchange which places the Doctor in the role of bystander and the gentlewoman as diagnostician:

Doctor	You see her eyes are open.
Gentlewoman	Ay, but their sense are shut.
Doctor	What is it she does now? Look how she rubs her hands.
Gentlewoman	It is an accustomed action with her, to seem thus washing her hands (5.1.23–8)

This is also not the only moment of female support that the play suggests. Lady Macbeth's suicide takes place out of sight, the only evidence of its occurrence the 'cry within of women' (5.5.7, s.d.). There is then aural, if not visual, evidence of other women surrounding Lady Macbeth, of a network which exists only within, and never onstage. These women (and the cry is very deliberately a cry of women, rather than the more usual 'noise within') offer, for a mere second, a collective mourning for a woman who is, while onstage and awake, never in female company. Yet, again, as with the gentlewoman and Doctor, the voices of the crying women are mediated by a male figure, Macbeth's servant Seyton, who explains their cry. Ultimately, the Doctor's only treatment for Lady Macbeth is further observation, a role which falls to the gentlewoman, who must 'still keep eyes upon her' (5.1.74). Under the intensity of this gaze, Lady Macbeth becomes the scene's optical focus, its 'vision'. The audience see her as a bloody apparition not unlike those seen by Macbeth in 4.1. Lady Macbeth's vision is then infectious in more ways than one; in her sleep, she becomes a spectre even before her own death: audiences see the vision of a future ghost walking.

Once her visions have begun, Lady Macbeth is pushed increasingly to the periphery. She is observed in her sleepwalking as if an actor; the audience never again see her awake or conscious of her visions. Following the vision scene, she remains offstage, mentioned briefly when Macbeth describes his wife's hallucinations as 'written troubles'. The sense of haunting images scored on the mind offers a particular understanding of the role of the visionary: trapped by the inevitable structure of tragedy, Lady Macbeth's fate is already written. Lady Macbeth is a spectator who cannot escape the play inside her head, watching her own scenes be performed again and again. Endlessly rotating back through the sounds ('knocking at the gate', 63–4), smells ('All the perfumes of Arabia will not sweeten this little hand', 48–9), and sights of the first four acts, by the fifth act Lady Macbeth is trapped, leaving only by the fail-safe exit from tragedy: death.

3.3 Conclusion

For Eleanor and Lady Macbeth, the vision cannot be easily separated from the anxieties and ambitions of the woman who experiences it. The vision becomes an expression of interiority, not only of inner dreams but of inner thoughts, standing alongside the soliloquy as an exteriorised articulation of self. The visions discussed in this section serve to expose an apparently frightening desire for power as well as a manifestation of mental illness. When Lady Macbeth and Eleanor speak it is, like many of the visionaries discussed here, in an attempt to intervene in their husband's political decisions. Richards and Thorne note that wives had a 'recognised duty to promote the interests and standing of their family' (2007: 14). In this sense, Eleanor and Lady Macbeth could be understood as exemplary spouses, if not exemplary subjects, putting their hopes and visions for their husband's future above the power structures of the monarchy. They are then perversions of ideal humanist wives: they might even be considered anti-wives, as the witch is often considered the anti-mother, who will ultimately destroy, not sustain, her husband.[15] They are active in political culture, using their husbands as proxy figures for their own ambition: the future they see is one in which they claim power through men. However, such attempts at power come at a price; like figures in a morality play, both women represent Ambition that must be curbed. The visions of future power that Eleanor describes and Lady Macbeth makes use of tell only half of the story: these visionaries are limited, too fixated on their rise to see the inevitable fall.

---

[15] See Willis (1995) and Purkiss (1996: 100–4) for discussion of this trope.

4 Believe Not Every Spirit

The term 'vision' serves to describe an array of imagined and hallucinated experiences precisely because of its semantic ambiguity: a vision is the term for both a sight seen and a sight imagined. It is ambiguity with which this section is concerned: the space for doubt created by the vision which is inherently unprovable as the only one with access to it is the visionary. A vision can be 'true' (divinely inspired) or 'false' (demonic), with no clear way to distinguish between the two. Referring to 2 Corinthians 11:14 ('And no marvel; for Satan himself is transformed into an angel of light'), Copeland and Machielsen emphasise the spiritual difficulty of believing even a vision experienced with one's own eyes: 'Paul's warning invites scepticism, calling on Christians to question the veracity and authenticity of what they perceive. But how were they to discern true content from the label on the box, especially when the two might be diametrically opposed and yet appear the same?' (2013: 2). It is this verse to which Holinshed refers in his description of the execution of Joan of Arc to argue that her visions are inherently untrustworthy: 'since Satan (after S. Paul) can change himself into an angel of light' (1587: 605). To see angels is no proof of divine inspiration if those angels might be devils in disguise. Once again, the truth of the vision is determined by how it is interpreted, not by its inherent value. After all, Joan was considered divinely inspired until she was no longer useful.

The visions discussed in this section are of devils and angels, although the distinction between the two is uncomfortably unclear. As Stuart Clark has discussed, the slippery semantic space between the demonic and divine has been a matter of considerable debate in discussions of visionary experience: 'Both good and bad angels could use their natural powers to alter the local motions of the animal spirits and humours which, in line with Aristotle's teaching in *De somniis*, caused the human phantasia to make images during sleep' (2007: 125). Moreover, while either devils or angels might induce a vision, there was further risk that the vision was a result of neither. Visions could be nothing more than mental images, created by a sleeping or disturbed mind. In *A Midsummer Night's Dream*, Theseus's definition of 'the lunatic' is one who experiences visions of devils: 'One sees more devils than vast hell can hold: / That is the madman' (5.1.9–10). Theseus's speech offers a model for the scepticism with which the demonic and angelic visions staged for Katherine and Joan are met. If such visions are a sign of madness, then the audience too are implicated, because, like the 'lunatic', playgoers see those spirits plainly.

4.1 Joan Puc/ʒel: Hearing Devils

In *1 Henry VI*, Joan Puc/zel is caught between the French for whom it is politically astute to believe that God is sending her favourable visions and the English who interpret those same visions as demonic.[16] Like Eleanor of Gloucester (discussed in Section 3), Joan is ultimately tried and punished for her apparent witchcraft. Shakespeare's Joan is 'Puzel or pussel' (Shakespeare, 2000: 1.4.106), the whore or the virgin; she is also Joan the witch, a 'railing Hecate' (3.5.24), or reanimated Medea (Stapleton, 1994: 231), whose military prowess is attributed to demonic influence. Yet, when that influence is at its most vital, it fails, and the fiends which flank Joan leave her in silence. Joan is a visionary whose visions desert her, a woman abandoned by the spectacular power for which she is executed.

Joan's first scene is one of visionary significance. Her first test of vision is to identify the Dauphin in a room of other men, a task she easily accomplishes. Standing before the Dauphin, itself a position of power accorded to no other woman in the play, Joan then describes the experience which called her to action: 'God's mother deignèd to appear to me, / And in a vision, full of majesty, / Willed me to leave my base vocation' (1.2.57–60). In recounting her vision, Joan's emphasis is on clarity. In her account, the Virgin Mary appears 'full of majesty' (58), suggesting that the image was sharp and complete. Its message is equally coherent, and Joan lays it out with precision. Still, Joan anticipates that she will not be believed and – before Charles replies – offers herself for trial by combat, understood in chivalric culture as

---

[16] Throughout, I refer to Joan Puc/zel, differing from the Oxford Shakespeare edition, which I otherwise cite, and which gives 'Joan la Pucelle' as speech prefix. The Folio offers both 'Puzel' (98) and 'Pucell' (107). I have therefore offered a hybrid name which neither damns Joan with a misogynistic slur nor sanitises the insult implied every time she is given lines to speak.

a sign from God, who would allow the righteous party to win (Russell, 2008: 335–57). Joan wins the fight and is finally given the status of prophetess. Her visionary power surpasses that of Helen, 'the mother of great Constantine' (121), whose vision of Christ led her to convert her son to Christianity, and that of 'Saint Philip's daughters' (122), all of whom were prophets (Acts 21:8–9). Charles's concession that she 'fightest with sword of Deborah' (1.2.84) aligns her clearly with 'a female judge, prophet, and war-leader' (Schroeder, 2014: 3). In the eyes of the Dauphin, at least, Joan is a visionary in the model of biblical visionaries: not only blessed by God but active in military command. Through the mention of these female visionaries – and, in the case of Deborah and Helen, their substantial political influence – Joan is established within a line of inspired women, her own visions given weight because of theirs. The need for such a list of ancestors does, however, suggest Joan's vulnerable position at court. Without such precedents, her word is not enough.

The devotion with which Charles receives Joan is held against the English reaction to her prophecies. Talbot implies that Joan's visions are intangible: 'So bees with smoke and doves with noisome stench / Are from their hives and houses driven away' (1.7.23–4). The smoke and smell of the visions and therefore Joan's effect on the English soldiers are mere airy tricks, nothing substantial. Smoke and smells are also the markers of stage lightning, the symbol of devils and witches (Thomson, 1999: 11–24). Joan's own arrival to battle against the English is marked with thunder as if she were a devil: even the English messenger's words that she is 'A holy prophetess, new risen up' (1.4.80) are suggestive of a devil rising from the hell space as much as of Joan's social ascension. As readily as the French raise Joan to the spiritual heights of biblical prophetesses, the English denigrate her through comparison to devils and witches. The stage directions of Joan's most explicit visionary moment in Act 5 offer an almost choral influence, pushing towards a demonic reading: Joan is visited by 'fiends' – she calls them 'choice' (5.3.3) and 'familiar spirits' (10) – who appear, by Joan's own admission, from 'powerful regions under earth' (11) in a moment of conjuring which aligns Joan with the persistent orientation towards the hell space in Eleanor's necromancy (see Section 3). In the one explicit glimpse given into Joan's visions, the audience learn that the visions are not in fact an unexpected revelation from God but rather summoned by Joan. The play which has so far fluctuated between English and French gazes – between Joan Puzel and Joan la Pucelle – now, jarringly, forces the audience's eyes firmly in one direction. Joan's visions are the result of witchcraft, not least because, as was held typical of witches, she is 'wont to feed [the fiends] with my blood' (14).[17] More degradingly still, Joan's witchcraft is no longer even potent in Act 5. The fiends 'walk and speak not' (12, s.d.), 'hang their heads' (17), 'shake their heads' (19). Her devils are not even the fiery, chatty, bombastic devils of the Medieval mystery plays: they are, as James Paxson has put it, 'diabolical mimes', ineffectual, even embarrassing (2001: 143).[18] Their silence suggests that Joan has no line of communication with the supernatural world beyond that created through her own delusion. Joan reacts to her silent devils with a phrase which parodies the Passion: Joan's 'See, they forsake me' (24) uncomfortably echoes the reported words of Christ on the cross, 'My God, my God, why hast thou forsaken me?' (Matthew 27: 46). Through this inversion, Joan's visions are reduced to petty conjuring as she suffers through a fifth act which 'dispe[ls] both Joan's power and her pretensions to divine aid in a series of progressively less dignified scenes' (Jackson, 1988: 41–2). In the play's penultimate scene, Joan is finally led offstage to be burned alive as a 'sorceress' (5.6.1), her visions now apparently confirmed false.

In her trial before the English, such as it is, Joan's word is twice called into doubt, firstly when she denies the lower-class shepherd parentage that she used to bolster her image earlier in the play, and secondly when she claims to be pregnant in the hope of being given a stay of execution. Robbed of all dignity, Joan dies as a liar, although her death provides her, for a moment, with an attentive English audience. Writing of women as witnesses in early modern England, Frances Dolan argues that the limits of female speech stretched until the point of death itself. Women at the point of execution were granted a rare opportunity to speak in public, but only as

---

[17] For more on this trope and further discussion of the 'polluting female body', see Purkiss (1996: 134).

[18] Maguire and Thomson's discussion of voice-hearing in *Doctor Faustus* offers an illuminating reading of a near contemporary play of *1 Henry VI* which stages demonic voices in terms of interiority and passivity (2020: 255–80).

they were about to be silenced by death (Dolan, 1994: 169). Yet, despite the illusion of agency in public speech, Joan's final words only induce confirmation bias: the inclination of the mind to gather evidence in favour of an already-held belief. Here, the men who already consider Joan to be 'Stained with the guiltless blood of innocents' (44) are primed to blame her every action. Realising that a fair hearing is impossible, Joan then turns to more earthly defences, only in her desperation finally foregrounding the gendered role that she has spent the play unwriting. In a seeming reversal of her position, she claims not to be a virgin after all, but to be pregnant, naming three possible fathers: the Dauphin, Alencon, and Reignier. Joan's final attempt to save her life seems the panicked reaction of a teenager about to face execution and serves to humiliate her further. Any of her claims that these men have fathered a child might be genuine; none can be proved. This ambiguity underscores the fraught relationship between prophecy and truth: if Joan will lie about this, the play suggests in its final moments of misogyny, she might lie about anything.

Further complicating the treatment of Shakespeare's Joan is the queerness of her gender representation: the historic Joan was, as Holinshed puts it in his list of her so-called misdeeds, charged with 'shamefully rejecting her sex abominably in acts and apparel to have counterfeited mankind, and then all damnably faithless, to be a pernicious instrument to hostility and bloodshed in devilish witchcraft and sorcery' (1587: 604).[19] The two charges are given equal weight: Joan is caught between an apparently counterfeit masculinity and the accusations of witchcraft used to undermine her speech when perceived as female. Sawyer Kemp has proposed that, in the context of justice-oriented pedagogy, 'We might model a close reading of Joan la Pucelle's madness through the lens of body dysphoria' (2019: 42), and certainly in her own lifetime Joan of Arc's gender identity was treated as

---

[19] My thinking here is indebted to Stryker, who offers a capacious definition of the term transgender as 'the movement across a socially imposed boundary away from an unchosen starting place, rather than any particular destination or mode of transition' (2008: 1). I am also indebted to the modelling of ways to 'fuse historicist methods with presentist concerns' expressed in *Early Modern Trans Studies* (Chess, Gordon, and Fisher, 2019: 11).

a matter for debate (Pernoud, 1964: 34–5). Joan's claim that she is pregnant is then more tragic still, as Joan negotiates the misogyny of the English by appealing to their fantasies of the female body as something that is knowable, controllable, and generative only through childbirth.[20] Ultimately, Joan is not only on trial for her visionary experiences, which are pre-emptively judged as witchcraft. Joan is put on trial for being an unknowable enemy. The English have no tolerance for ambiguity: Joan's 'puzzling body' (Spiess, 2016: 106) cannot be explained, her visions cannot be proved, and so she is removed from their version of history.

Joan's battle to be heard has been examined recently in Charlie Josephine's *I, Joan* (2022), a powerful response to *1 Henry VI* which speaks in defence of self-identification and the rights of trans and non-binary people. In the play's complicated representation of visionary experience, Joan's (Isobel Thom) visions are more often described as innate and self-generated, and even when they do seem to come from God, they are not images so much as instincts, a sense of a 'calling' or 'Truth'.[21] This shift, away from the Joan in *1 Henry VI* who describes specific images of the Virgin Mary and is later shown to the audience surrounded by devils, cuts to the question of what the vision is and how (indeed, if) it can be proved. *I, Joan* does not stage its visions for public scrutiny because the opinion of others has no bearing on what is true to Joan, who urges that 'everyone would listen to their insides, for there the Kingdom of Heaven sings sweetly' (13). The play makes clear that access to divine truth comes through knowledge of oneself: it is felt, not seen.

Despite the play's representation of vision as an experience which can sometimes be drawn from within and which needs no external proof, Joan is not believed. Joan, who moves in and out of the world of the play, often

---

[20] While Holinshed's account suggests that the claim of pregnancy 'gave her nine months stay' from execution, 'at the end whereof she found herein as false as wicked' (1587: 604), Shakespeare's York gives Joan neither credence nor time, meaning that the pregnancy is not proved false before Joan is taken to her death.

[21] 'Prompt Book for *I, Joan*', GB 3316 SGT / THTR / SM / 1 / 2022 / IJ; all text and page numbers for *I, Joan* are taken from this prompt book, with thanks to Shakespeare's Globe.

addressing the audience directly, first interacts with Charles, the Dauphin, three generic male advisors (Man One, Man Two, and Man Three), and Thomas, another advisor, who, throughout the play, will try to understand Joan as both visionary leader and non-binary person. In this scene, when Charles expresses excitement at Joan's arrival (not because he takes them seriously but because he is bored), his advisors offer paint-by-numbers misogyny (assuming, as they do, that the 'strange visitor' arriving is a 'girl on horseback' (8)):

MAN TWO:	But sir! She could be a fraud!
MAN ONE:	Or a mad woman! An assassin!
MAN TWO:	Or a witch!
MAN ONE:	Or the devil himself!
CHARLES:	Or a monster from the deep dark depths of foolish man's imagination?! She's a *girl*! A simple *maid*! I want to meet with her. (8)

Joan might be a con artist or a devil, rapt and out of control or viciously calculating. Yet, refreshingly, given the constant interrogations which make up *1 Henry VI*, Joan's origin story is never fully put to the test in a scene which shows no interest in pandering to or disproving these accusations. Instead, Joan quickly recognises the king in disguise, but, in another move away from the narrative of *1 Henry VI*, all details of their visions are stripped away and are discussed only offstage. Joan announces, 'I have been sent by God to deliver a message to you' (9) but offers their message to Charles alone and asks for privacy. Here, Joan moves from a central stage position to an offstage space, and those onstage are left to wait. Yet, even proximity to a visionary moment is staged as a kinetic reaction, a physical shudder shared by the men waiting onstage who 'begin shaking'.[22] The erratic movement, which reads as a physical resistance to taking in Joan's truth, is repeated in Joan's final trial scene. Again, in Joan's presence, judges move and jerk like clockwork automata to the sound of rattling and knocking percussion, interrupting and repeating themselves incessantly. It

---

[22] Handwritten note for p. 13 of promptbook.

is as if Joan's visions, never staged for the audience's judgement, cannot be fully absorbed by these sceptical bodies which instead shudder with resistance. Joan's visions come from inside their own body; such intangible truths will not be accepted by the bodies of their judges.

In the first act of the play, Joan is sometimes believed, but that belief is contingent not only on their success and cooperation but on the court's limited understandings of gender identity. Most shockingly in the play, Joan's early supporters, Charles's wife and mother, Marie and Yolande, who are framed as powerful proxy-rulers, who 'hold the purse strings' (20) and 'advise these men who sit safely in the palm of my hand', viciously retract support when Joan refuses to wear a perceived marker of femininity, a pink dress. Charles's support is also retracted when he considers Joan to have outlived their usefulness. This anxiety is expressed as an envy of their visions: 'I am the *King*! Why does God not send his messages to me?!' (60). Elsewhere, Charles simply 'covers his ears' (77) to Joan's moans of pain. In the play's second act, Joan's relationship with Charles is fractured, as Charles no longer allows them access to his presence: the exclusivity of Joan's offstage visions, told to Charles in private, are now horribly echoed in their exclusion from the court. *I, Joan* stages the unsettling reality of contingent belief, demonstrating the ways in which Joan is accepted so long as their visions support the agenda or biases of the politicians around them. Without showing a vision onstage, the play offers a radical challenge: believe people when they speak about their own experiences, whether or not those experiences seem tangible or are made visible.

This challenge extends to the structure of the play itself. *I, Joan* uses the metatheatrical power of the vision to resist its apparently forewritten conclusion. Many of the visions discussed in this study seem true as soon as they are spoken because they express what is now historical fact, such as the death of Caesar. This Joan can see the end of their play and tries to resist it with the simple choice, 'fuck your historically accurate … Joan aint dying tonight!' (88). Yet, their vision of 'how my story ends' (86) plays out nonetheless: in an echo of Joan's claims of pregnancy in *1 Henry VI*, Josephine's Joan disavows their visions under the threat of fire and is ultimately taken from the stage to be executed. The visionary intervention that Joan makes in the play's final scenes is not then to change the ending of the story but the way it is told, as a Girl remains onstage, cutting her hair in imitation of Joan and singing to lead a 'joyous rebellion of bodies moving together' (92). *I, Joan* does not argue that our retrospective gaze can change the performance of the past, but it does provide a vision of what might have been, an experience of Joan's contagious alternative reality.

4.2 Katherine of Aragon: Seeing Angels

Shakespeare and Fletcher's *Henry VIII* is predicated on prophecies, ending with a final prediction from Cranmer that King Henry's daughter will become the Virgin Queen, Elizabeth I, and will herself be succeeded by James VI/I. This 'oracle of comfort' (5.4.66) seems to conclude the history play neatly, drawing its lines of influence right up to the present, Jacobean day. Yet, despite the lofty proclamations of Cranmer, the only substantive vision of the play belongs to Katherine, the rejected, Catholic, Spanish former queen, a woman who is, at the moment of the vision, too infirm to stand unaided. Katherine's vision of six white-clad figures is performed before the audience's eyes. Her experience, unlike any other in Shakespeare, is specifically called 'The vision', a title printed in the Folio. Yet, vision is a slippery term, one which invokes both truth and delusion, actual sight and imagined sensation: is this what Katherine 'sees' as she dreams or is some higher, psychic sense of 'see' invoked? By 'meditating' (4.2.79) to music which she terms her 'knell' (79), Katherine has established the cognitive conditions in which a vivid dream might be induced. She thinks of 'that celestial harmony I go to' (80), creating the kind of mental fixation thought to frame the content of dreams. The vision itself, even if only a manifestation of Katherine's final thoughts, is a last, passive, if no less important, example of her political role throughout the play. In her first scene, Katherine intervenes to challenge Wolsey's policy and question the king's decision on taxes; she later defends herself at her divorce trial and refuses to adhere to the court's judgement. This is a queen who has shown herself to be an active agent, speaking on her own behalf as well as on that of the people. Here, in the vision, she is silent as she seems to receive divine approval for her decisions, and especially for her refusal to accept divorce as a devout Catholic. Even if the vision is a dream, conjured from her inner meditations, it reflects a sense of peace in her own decisions.

However, the stage directions betray a hesitation in their parenthetical instructions for Katherine: 'At which (as it were by inspiration) she makes in her sleep signs of rejoicing and holds up her hands to heaven' (82, s.d.). The language is ambiguous: 'as it were' might suggest either 'as by inspiration' or the more subjective 'as if by inspiration'. The audience are left to read Katherine's body, interpreting her 'signs of rejoicing'. It is only after the vision that the audience learn that Katherine's movements were perhaps part of the vision and did not take place in reality: neither Griffith nor Patience, who have sat in attendance, saw any sign of them (or, at least, understood their meaning). Whatever tangible proof there might be is left behind within the vision world: the crown which Katherine is given is removed, as the dancers 'vanish, carrying the garland with them' (82, s.d.). The conditions of the vision (Katherine is explicitly asleep) tempt the audience to consider it as merely a dream (where readers may know it as a 'vision', playgoers do not). This, certainly, is Griffith's assumption as Katherine describes her vision: 'I am most joyful, madam, such good dreams / Possess your fancy' (4.2.94–5). Unable to see what Katherine (and, crucially, the audience) have seen, Griffith assumes that the parade of white-clad personages represents only the workings of Katherine's sleeping mind. Funlola Olufunwa offered the following insight into playing Katherine of Aragon (as she did in a rehearsed reading I directed for Creation Theatre in 2020).[23] Speaking of Katherine's evident illness in her last scene, Olufunwa suggests, 'Her mind was working to comfort her. There was also some disjointed thinking, because one minute there's music, then there isn't. The human mind, it does that, doesn't it?' (Personal interview, 2021).[24] The scene foregrounds not only Katherine's

---

[23] https://www.youtube.com/watch?v=BFMh1jzzB9w.

[24] I am indebted to Funlola for also taking the time to speak to me about her own play, *Keeping up with Kassandra* (dir. Anne Musisi, 2021), which draws on Cassandra's role in the *Iliad* to consider intersectional questions of class, race, and mental illness as they connect with ideas of prophetic female speech in an era of 'bad, fake news'. Kassandra's (Diana Yekinni) knowledge of the future is held suspect because 'she is a woman and an African woman at that', because she is 'an inconvenient truth-teller, and that comes at a price'. Kassandra, who 'hinted on live television that she was pregnant' before her final broadcast, also offers

bodily vulnerability (her legs are 'loaded branches' now 'Willing to leave their burden', 3–4), but a mind failing through forgetfulness and pain. As the scene begins, she has already been told of Wolsey's death, but needs Griffith to tell her again. The same uncertainty is evident after Katherine's vision: 'Saw you not even now a blessèd troop / Invite me to a banquet . . .?' (4.2.87–8). Her perception of the world is already compromised, her memory faulty, and this fraying mental state casts doubt upon the vision itself. The vision is tied to Katherine's failing body, which 'is altered on the sudden', 'pale' and 'earthly cold' (97–9). Yet, the vision is also a balm for her anxiety, and seems to be followed by an earthly blessing to match the perceived divine blessing: a final kind word from her husband, Henry, sent by messenger even as the white-clad personages might be messengers from God. Even if it exists only in Katherine's mind, the dumb show of the vision is Shakespeare's most extended reverie on what might happen after death, his theatricalisation of the divinely ordained fate awaiting this queen.

In a far more theatrically experimental vision than the described dreams I have discussed elsewhere, Shakespeare allows his audience to see the spectacle of Katherine's vision. In her vision, Katherine is offered the crown she has been denied through the divorce proceedings staged in Act 3. The dancers hold a garland over her head, its bay leaves suggestive of victory. E. E. Duncan-Jones suggests that this represents the '"crown of life", promised to those "faithful unto death"' (1961: 142). Certainly, the Book of Revelation promises: 'ye shall have tribulation ten days: be thou faithful unto death, and I will give thee a crown of life' (2:10). The garland of bay leaves serves as the crown Katherine, named explicitly as 'Dowager' in the stage directions (4.2.1, s.d.) has lost. As I have discussed elsewhere (Wright, 2021: 289), the crown also recalls the bay branches brought to Elizabeth I in Spenser's *The Shepherd's Calendar* (1579), aligning the two monarchs despite the fact that Anne Bullen, not Katherine, is Elizabeth's mother. The vision scene is one of redemption but also of vindication. Katherine's dream comes moments after she has learned of

a fascinating parallel with Shakespeare's Joan Puc/zel. The play exposes urgent questions of misogynoir and ableism (Kassandra is epileptic) in the casting and performance of visionary women in and beyond Shakespeare: see creationthea-tre.co.uk/show/kassandra/.

her great enemy, Wolsey's, death, and now she seems to go to her own, shepherded by divine spirits who address the damage done to her by offering her a divine crown in place of a royal one.

The vision is, however, ambiguous enough to leave Katherine's fate in some doubt. The 'six personages clad in white robes' (4.2.82, s.d.) might suggest angels; certainly, there is biblical precedent for the manifestation of angels in white, when Mary Magdalene 'looked into the sepulchre, And seeth two angels in white sitting, the one at the head, and the other at the feet, where the body of Jesus had lain' (John 20:11–12). The iconography of white robes also firmly aligns Katherine with purity when the validity of her marriage has been tried in court. It is the colour not only of the goddess Vesta, 'clad in white purity', Daniel, 1604: B1v) but of Queen Elizabeth I, 'Clad in the Virgin ornament of white' (Lever, 1607: B1r). Yet, within Shakespeare's plays, white robes are also theatrically haunted, weighted with darker associations.[25] White is the colour of Eleanor's shrift ('white sheet', 2.4.17, s.d.) in *2 Henry VI*, as she is paraded through the streets. The visual ambiguity of the personages is also complicated by the 'golden vizards' (82, s.d.) they wear, not least as, proverbially, golden vizards often concealed leaden faces. Even this ambiguous proverb is, itself, ambiguous. William Fulbeck uses the proverb in discussing those who shield themselves with a more powerful patron: 'so having gotten a golden vizard to a bad face, he thinketh he may mask in all kind of pleasures' (1587: D7v). Yet, John Norden condemns Catholics who misinterpret the Word of God by turning to that same proverb: 'they have a golden vizard upon their leaden faces, they have the names but not the effect or fruits of Catholics' (1586: 24). This ambivalence is an idea Katherine has already invoked in her criticism of Wolsey: 'Ye have angels' faces, but heaven knows your hearts' (3.1.144). The masked personages in her vision are uncertain: they are either the true

---

[25] This association lingers beyond the early modern stage. See, for instance Barish's discussion of the use of colour: 'A further link between madness and the somnambulism of Lady Macbeth would seem to be suggested in the eighteenth century by the fact that Mrs Siddons, the most celebrated Lady Macbeth of the day, performed the sleepwalking scene in white satin. This, to at least one observer, indicated lunacy' (1984: 151).

faces of angels or a cruel delusion, an echo of Wolsey, who hid behind the mask of Henry.

Katherine's vision is also an echo and inversion of a scene in Heywood's *If You Know Not Me, You Know Nobody* (1605), in which a dumb-show dream is shown to the princess who will become Elizabeth I in her sleep. In both plays, the queen calls for music and falls asleep, witnesses figures, and wakes to find her maid has seen and heard nothing. In Heywood, a 'dumb show' of two angels is also made up of political players such as Winchester (E4v); in Shakespeare and Fletcher, Katherine is alone with her angels. Elizabeth's dumb show offers protection against a Catholic figure (the angels shield her from a friar who is 'offering to kill her'), emphasised by the open Bible that is placed in her hands. Katherine is given, instead, garlands, which emphasise her own spiritual value: if read as a riposte to Heywood's Protestant fantasy of the Word, Katherine's vision emerges as a paean to personal Catholic faith.[26] Yet, at all turns – in resisting naming the figures onstage as angels, and in refusing to allow Katherine the evidence of her garland (Elizabeth keeps her Bible as proof of the experience) – Shakespeare and Fletcher offer ambiguity. Katherine is aligned with Heywood's Elizabeth through this echo but is not given the clear message that Elizabeth receives (the Bible left in her hands is open to the verse 'Whoso putteth his trust in the Lord / Shall not be confounded', E4r). Katherine's vision offers no evidence, but it does end with some validation of her faith: she does not receive instructions for the future but a reward for the past, dying as she does with an apparent mark of divine approval. This divine approval is, however, not entirely clear. As Mira Kafantaris has shown, Katherine's vision cannot be straightforwardly cate-gorised according to the play's own desired demarcations of faith: 'Catholic as she undoubtedly is, Katherine does experience a vision on her deathbed of Protestant piety. Her vision, unfolding through a set of elaborate stage directions, speaks to the inner experience of direct revelation, which the

---

[26] In describing the inconstancy of human affection in *Religio Medici*, Thomas Browne treats the dumb show and dream as synonymous, and as equally fallacious: 'Let us call to assize the lives of our parents, the affection of our wives and children, and they are all dumb shows, and dreams without reality, truth, or constancy' (1642: 157–8).

reformation heralded' (2018: 340). While the vision may attest to Katherine's own piety, it does not answer the play's debates over the value of different kinds of Christian faith. Although Katherine's vision is staged at length, it is on the prediction of the newly born, Protestant Elizabeth I's glorious reign that the play ends.

For all her infirmity, the vision seems to reaffirm Katherine's belief in her own historical place. Although the 'blessèd troop' (87) bring Katherine garlands she is 'not worthy yet to wear' (92), by the end of the scene Katherine has reclaimed confidence enough to insist that she is buried with 'maiden flowers' (170), and 'although unqueened, yet like / A queen and daughter to a king' (172–3). For Katherine, as Catholic queen, the vision which appears as her death approaches might be a sign of virtue and martyrdom: 'Catholic martyrologists also used dreams to demonstrate that those who died had been shown by God that they were heroes who should meet death with serenity' (Levin, 2008: 67). It is peace, not political or spiritual influence, that the vision offers. Ultimately, Katherine's vision pulls against the historical narrative which would frame her death as miserable and inconsequential, removed from the attention of court. Whether this is a divine message, or whether it is a dream as Katherine convinces herself that she is saved, the vision's effect is the same: it gives Katherine the strength at this final moment to die with dignity, forgiving Henry and insisting on the royal trappings of burial. Through this reclamation of her own crown, Katherine reasserts her position as queen and denies the temporary indignity of her position as dowager for a queenly monument in futurity.

4.3 Conclusion

Waking, Joan sees devils; sleeping, Katherine sees angels. Yet, despite what should be a clear distinction between the hellish and the heavenly, the two spectacles are worryingly similar. In both, silent figures visit the visionary in a dumb show to which the audience also has access. These visions appear to offer clarity – *look, here are figures of evil or of good!* – but instead offer ambiguity. Even those visions which are staged rather than recounted are troubling speculative rather than confidently spectacular. They require interrogation, but interrogation is not easy, in part because visions leave behind no trace. Although they have shared their vision with an audience, Katherine and Joan have no proof beyond their own testimony: Katherine, as I discussed earlier, is not permitted to hold onto her crown of bay as Heywood's Elizabeth holds on to her Bible. And the existence of tangible evidence might make little difference anyway.

James VI/I's manifesto on witchcraft, *Daemonology* (1597), which insists that visions are the work of the devil, takes pains to dismiss even physical evidence of such experiences. In their dialogue, Philomathes and Epistemon speak about a vision of a fairyland, a dream from which witches return carrying a small stone in their hand as proof that their experience was real. Epistemon explains away the stone:

> For may not the devil object to their fantasy, their senses being dulled, and as it were asleep, such hills and houses within them, such glistering courts and trains, and whatsoever such like wherewith he pleaseth to delude them. And in the meantime their bodies being senseless, to convey in their hand any stone or such like thing, which he makes them to imagine to have received in such a place. (James VI, 1597: 74–5)

While the mind is vulnerable and sleeping (or as if asleep), the devil might suggest any number of sights which would seem true. Even a stone, brought back as proof of a visionary experience, is dismissed as a trick played upon a body which is 'senseless' (although not innocent, as James makes clear that visionary women are witches). Even Shakespeare's most explicit visions offer no surety: the audience watch Katherine and Joan and feel an illusion of sensory solidarity, but this is immediately undermined by the fact that no one else within the play world shares the vision. Evidence is not enough: no proof will satisfy a listener who is determined not to hear. If the playgoer thinks Katherine is saved, her dream is a vision; if they believe in Joan, she is taunted by devils but not controlled by them. Like a religious icon, a vision becomes an image made meaningful through meditation, an object of reflection which demands faith rather than generating it.

5 Sooth-Dreams

This section is concerned with visions that are seen while waking, visions that offer an almost tangible experience of death that has not yet come. Both Margaret, discussed above as a threat to Eleanor in *2 Henry VI*, and Constance, the mother of Arthur, a claimant to the throne in *King John*, speak and think in a future-oriented manner: they draw on the evidence of the past to predict the outcomes of the future, in a way that uses the language and trappings of the vision even if it is not precisely visionary. Their experiences of imagined grief are, to borrow a phrase from James I's *Daemonology*, 'sooth-dreams', or waking visions, described in the same passage as that discussed at the conclusion of Section 4, which claims that visions are experienced by women deluded that they have visited a fairyland: 'But what say ye to their foretelling the death of sundry persons, whom they allege to have seen in these places? That is, a sooth-dream (as they say) since they see it walking' (1597: 75).

In this visionary state, women see the dead, not as a ghost but as an apparition of a living person who will soon die. The grammar here is unclear: is the visionary walking (and presumably waking) or is the spirit? Both the visions I discuss here play out not during sleep itself but during moments of semi-lucid grief. Both experience panic as much as prophecy, fixated as they are on what will come. There is, however, something predictive about Margaret and Constance's visionary thoughts of future death: their sooth-dreams are fear made real through imagination and, crucially, fear that proves true.

Margaret of Anjou, whose presence is felt across Shakespeare's first tetralogy, offers sibyl-like speeches promising that the chain of deaths across these history plays will continue. Her curses contain the seeds of visions which are expanded in later plays: her preoccupation with death offers the model for Constance's hyper-sensory experience of grief. Both Margaret and Constance's roles are dominated by maternal grief: there is a troubling implication that women's bodies are so intimately tied to the future in generating offspring that prophetic experiences take the place of lost motherhood as a way to reach forward in time. Margaret's prediction that she will one day be considered a 'prophetess' (1.3.299), 'scor[ned] for my gentle counsel' (295) also frames her as a prototype of Cassandra, who faces hostility for her future-gazing later in Shakespeare's career (see Section 2). In Margaret's case, the sheer will for revenge appears to make her curses manifest: or, perhaps, her curses only reflect that which is inevitable in a historical cycle of destruction. Yet, despite these repeated musings on death, neither Margaret nor Constance is an abstract figure of grief: they intercede, argue, and protest, witnesses to the past and future, active in the present.

The imagined visions (visionary imaginings?) of Constance blur the semantic distinction between hope and foresight. Both Margaret and Constance see a future formed not from external influences, demonic or divine, but from the fixations of their own minds. Margaret imagines an endless cycle of death and prophesises doom for the living; Constance too sees her son caught between life and death, potentially gone. Death itself, which is at once so grimly visual – as the ghostly clothes Constance imagines filled with her son's body suggest – and at the same time, beyond the veil of sight, becomes a locus for thought which, if not visionary, brushes closely against that mode. In her discussion of the 'ocular sublime', Suzannah Biernoff has described the ways in which 'vision is inextricably bound up with desire' as 'a state of suspension on the threshold between self and other' (2002: 132). The intangible experience of death is something Margaret rehearses through active envisioning, just as Constance negotiates her ghost-less grief by creating a phantom in her mind. Their sooth-dreams (or visions of those who will die) are of their own making. The mind becomes a stage on which to rehearse visionary experience: in the end, Margaret and Constance see internally, creating meaning through the images in their heads.

5.1 Queen Margaret: Predictive Memory

The Margaret briefly discussed in Section 3, who organises the trap that will see Eleanor arrested for necromancy, is not quite the same Margaret discussed here, who reappears, ahistorically, in *Richard III*, to serve as both reminder of the past and prophet of future doom. This Margaret (who should, technically, be exiled in France) is brought back as a walking memory, a living ghost who intrudes into the present. Yet, as a walking memory, the Margaret of *Richard III* carries with her the weight of her past iterations. In *2 Henry VI*, following the humiliation of Eleanor discussed above, Margaret explains the difficulties of expressing her political opinion, using the tropes levied against women's speech to add weight to her own. Following a lengthy and articulate answer as to Gloucester's current whereabouts (thirteen times the length of Henry's question), Margaret turns typical accusations against women's speech on their head to bolster her own argument:

> If it be fond, call it a woman's fear;
> Which fear if better reasons can supplant,
> . . . Reprove my allegation, if you can;
> Or else conclude my words effectual. (3.1.36–41)

Margaret links fondness with 'women's fear', but this is not the dismissal it may seem. If her words are silly, they can be considered the fault of her sex, but women's fears were also believed to carry a particular weight as well as a particular weakness: women are silly and hysterical, or else highly intuitive. The problematic phenomenon of 'female intuition' is still very much in circulation today and serves to masculinise its opposite, logic.[27] In her speech, Margaret uses the distinction between fear and reason to place the burden of disproving her words on Henry: if he cannot, he must believe her worries about Gloucester. The rhetorical trick means that Margaret is required to provide no evidence while Henry must find positive proof of Gloucester's loyalty, a task that is impossible as it would require knowing not only Gloucester's actions but his thoughts.

---

[27] The problem of attributing intuition to women (and, by doing so, dismissing their reason) is perhaps most famously captured by a remark from Prime Minister Stanley Baldwin who, 'when defending the extension of the franchise to women of 21, said, "I have not a profound confidence in feminine logic, but I have in feminine instinct".' This comment was quoted and challenged in a 1927 study that showed no difference between male and female instincts (although that study is itself no longer adequate, dependent as it was on physiognomy): www.theguardian.com/theguardian/2012/sep/07/womens-intuition-myth-tested-archive-1927.

Margaret negotiates a world in which neither she nor the idea of prophecy is taken seriously. *Richard III*, for instance, begins with a demonstration that prophecy can be manipulated or made up for political ends. Richard has used 'drunken prophecies, libels and dreams' (1.1.33) to pit his brothers Clarence and King Edward IV, against one another, and will use 'a prophecy which says that "G" / Of Edward's heirs the murderer shall be' (39–40) to facilitate his brother's arrest and murder. At first, it seems that Margaret's role is not one of future-gazing but of 'repetition of what [Richard] has marred' (1.3.165); she is fixated on the past and on re-enacting its violence in the present. If there are prophecies, she is their subject. As Dorset warns her, recalling her involvement in the death of Rutland, 'No man but prophesised revenge for it' (1.3.183). Prophecies are treated as promises: a desire to bend the future rather than a vision of the future. The conflation is expressed by Margaret: 'dire induction am I witness to, / And will to France' (4.4.5–6). The vision is caught between the two, witness and will, as a vengeful future that can be both intuited and enacted.

Margaret's role in *Richard III* is not only to curse but to stir other women to cursing: those curses then morph retrospectively into predictions, as they prove true by the end of the play. In *Richard III*, her first entrance is as 'old Queen Margaret, unseen behind them' (1.3.109, s.d.). Both the description of her character and her position onstage show that her role is as a figure of the past: hovering behind those who are still actively engaged with politics, Margaret becomes the embodiment of memory while insisting on vengeance in the future. In this way, Margaret raises a troubling question: must a visionary always look forwards? Nonetheless, despite the thoughts which draw her back into the past, Margaret speaks in the future tense, warning Queen Elizabeth that 'The day will come that thou shalt wish for me / To help thee curse this poisonous bunch-backed toad' (1.3.243–4). Her curses are something that can be taught, as Elizabeth eventually learns. With the request, 'teach me how to curse mine enemies' (4.4.117), Elizabeth reveals her own intuition that Margaret's curses are going to be made real. She also acknowledges Margaret's visionary role, admitting that her warnings have come true and repeating Margaret's words as if to give them the weight of an incantation:

> O thou did prophesy the time would come
> That I should wish for thee to help me curse
> That bottled spider, that foul bunch-backed toad. (4.4.79–81)

Elizabeth finally believes Margaret's capacity to intuit the future and now, rather than scorning it, as she has throughout the play, asks for similar insight. Despite (or, perhaps, because of) Richard's obvious disdain for women, *Richard III* is interested in the ways in which women understand each other and share their recourse to ill wishes if not to actual revenge. In a scene that is later echoed in *King John* (discussed in the next section), Margaret is held beside another grieving mother, the Duchess of York, who describes herself as a walking vision of the past:

> Brief abstract and record of tedious days,
> Rest thy unrest on England's lawful earth,
> Unlawfully made drunk with innocents' blood! (4.4.28–30)

The Duchess of York is soon joined by both Queen Elizabeth and, in surprising solidarity, Margaret herself. They sit together as if unable to move forward by playing their part any longer. Instead, they create a pause, a moment of powerful stillness in the present from which they can observe the past and future. These women share the role of 'abstract' for their time, recalling and embodying the recent political past in a world which seems to move so quickly between wars that former losses are forgotten. For a moment, these mothers are made static by their grief, able to claim only the space where they sit. Knowledge of the future is not the same as agency; unable to act, they think revenge on the men around them, imagining deaths to wash away past deaths.

This solidarity between women who find no place in the present is drawn out in Jeanie O'Hare's rewritten history, *Queen Margaret* (2018). O'Hare crafts a character who is supported only by her continual conversation with Joan of Arc, who exists for Margaret as something between vision, memory, and ghost. Margaret and Joan overlap in their visionary fates in a detail not drawn from Shakespeare: in O'Hare, Margaret was brought to Joan's execution as a baby and was 'the last sound [Joan] heard on this earth'

(21). Their connection in this sense is historic. Margaret's mother, O'Hare stresses, was Joan's patron: 'Margaret would have grown up witnessing political machinations, thinking about Joan morning, noon and night' (2018: 6). In each other, O'Hare's Joan and Margaret find a confidante, even if only in an intangible form, as Margaret remembers or hallucinates Joan long after her death. O'Hare's Margaret is herself a visionary who reads moments retrospectively, pinning down meaning only once events have taken place, as shown in her lament to Joan: 'This bloody wound may make some sense to us tomorrow' (87). In this, there is also a flickering allusion to Calphurnia, whose bloody dream is proved correct only in retrospect, when tomorrow has come on the Ides of March. This is how Margaret's visionary sight operates, looking backwards and forwards, shedding light on the present only through the lenses of other times.

In *Queen Margaret*, both Margaret and Joan twist in and out of their prescribed Shakespearean roles. O'Hare draws on scenes from across the first tetralogy to present a Margaret who demands active political influence, laid out boldly in such scene titles as 'Scene Four – Margaret Encourages the King to Rule' (26). Yet, even in this scene, Margaret is positioned on the edges of political power, a kingmaker in the only way a woman apparently can be: a mother of heirs, whose child is brought onstage as the scene comes to a close. It is only at the end of Act 1 that Margaret is a more active agent, taking the dagger offered to her by Joan with which she will ultimately slit York's throat. Margaret is told by the vision of Joan that she acts with divine authority: 'All the power of heaven is now behind you!' (69). Yet, Joan's words are suspect, not least because Joan herself, a walking ghost in 'purgatory' (93), echoes the visionary experiences of Joan Puc/zel. O'Hare's Joan takes the role of the silent devils who patrolled around Joan in *1 Henry VI*. In 1.9, O'Hare's Margaret asks Joan to answer as she paces the stage but '*Joan remains silent*' (43), even as Joan in *1 Henry VI* is ignored by her own pacing devils. The scene offers a moment of split vision: those familiar with Shakespeare's play will see an allusion that casts O'Hare's Joan in a more troubling light. As with all visions, interpretation is shaped by prior knowledge and prejudices.

Through the spirit of Joan, Margaret is a visionary who sees the past but not the future, her thoughts tied to a memory, ghost, or hallucination who offers no details of what will come. When Joan 'conjures' Warwick's death for Margaret (93), it has already happened. For all Margaret sees, she is never sure of her own prophetic power. *Queen Margaret* ends with just this question; as she leaves England for France, Margaret wonders, 'But maybe I am a prophet' (100). If so, Richard of York will kill his brother Edward and assume the role of king. Audiences know from history and from Shakespeare that this will prove true in *Richard III*. O'Hare's Margaret is a visionary who imagines how her story will play out: she is, like playgoers, conscious of a relentless historical tide which is, from her position, the future. Shakespeare's Margaret returns to see the show, watching her curses come to pass as much through the inevitability of violence as of her visions.

5.2 Queen Constance: Proleptic Grief

For the first part of *King John*, Constance is a political player, fighting for her son's claim to the English throne. Constance refuses to accept a political marriage between John's niece and the Dauphin which damages Constance's son Arthur's claim. Yet, Constance is widely dismissed. Constance has already been treated by her mother-in-law, Queen Eleanor, and by her son, Arthur, as a hysterical, slanderous figure. In her first scene she is cut short both by King John with the dismissive, 'Bedlam, have done' (2.1.183) and by King Philip with the curt line, 'Peace, lady: pause or be more temperate' (2.1.195). Yet, Constance is so widely criticised for speaking up on behalf of Arthur's claim to the throne not because she is hysterical but because she is correct. Her advocacy on behalf of her son's claim must be deemed mad or else it might work. This constant critique of Constance's word is, finally, invoked by her and turned on its head, just as Margaret uses her 'woman's fear' as a rhetorical tool above. Dismissing Salisbury's word of the political marriage between the Dauphin and Blanche, Constance insists:

> Thou shalt be punished for thus frightening me;
> For I am sick and capable of fears;
> Oppressed with wrongs and therefore full of fears;
> A widow husbandless, subject to fears;
> A woman naturally born to fears. (2.2.11–15)

Constance frames herself as a woman who is prone to paranoia, worrying constantly about what might happen. Yet Constance's grief is not a weakness: it is the source of both her visionary experience and her acts of protest. Just as Margaret marshals her sorrow ('Think therefore on revenge and cease to weep', *2 Henry VI*, 4.4.3)), Constance insists that she will use her emotions rather than suppress them: 'I shall instruct my sorrows to be proud, / For grief is proud and makes his owner stoop' (68–9). This pride takes the form of what might now be called a sit-down protest, as Constance takes the ground for her 'throne' (74) and refuses to move (at least for a moment). It is a direct echo of the scene in *Richard III*, discussed above, in which three women sit on the ground and share their grief, momentarily stepping out of action. Yet, Constance does not remain motionless. When she does stand, it is to contradict King Philip with curses and then to end her protest with a line that is painfully typical of visionary women: 'Hear me, O hear me!' (3.1.38).

Despite the protest and the rage that Constance expresses on her son's behalf in the first acts of the play, Constance's role shifts when, with her fear of Arthur's death, she is no longer able to see a future and instead envisages one. Following news of her son's imprisonment, Constance sees her child everywhere as a waking dream. Constance grieves sincerely, believing Arthur will soon die, but, unlike Hamlet or Macbeth who see ghosts that might be real or might be imagined, Constance definitely cannot actually see her son's ghost. He is, after all, still alive. He exists to her only as a vision, imagined internally, not encountered. Yet, even as loss makes Constance appear to look inwards, she speaks out; even as she appears to look backwards, she is actually looking ahead, imagining how Arthur 'will look as hollow as a ghost' (3.4.84). Constance dominates her 'vision' scene, which is positioned at roughly the centre of *King John* and is played before a hostile male audience (King Philip, Lewis, Cardinal Pandolf, and male attendants are present). It is as if her grief splices the play into before (with Arthur) and after (without him), insisting that this play be constructed around her own political hopes. Yet, Constance's visionary experience becomes a false temporal marker, undermined by the presence of Arthur, alive, in the following scene.

Constance becomes a prophetic harbinger, warning of a death which is inevitable not only because of Arthur's imprisonment but because he is a bit player in a historical plot and his fate is already written. In mental distress,

Constance fabricates a sensory experience to replace the actual absence of Arthur: grief is that which 'fills the room up of my absent child' (3.4.93). Constance's experience of Arthur is part memory (the image 'Remembers me of all his gracious parts', 95) and part ghost, almost corporeal in that it 'Stuffs out his vacant garments with his form' (97). Constance is imagining future grief, playing out her mourning before it happens; for Pandolf, who hears her with disdain, this is 'madness, and not sorrow' (43). Constance moves from future imaginings of resurrection to a present tense imagination in which Grief 'walks up and down with me' (94) as a constant companion. This temporal disjunction positions Constance not as a grieving mother but as a visionary seeing future death. Arthur, of course, does die in 4.3, leaping from the walls moments after King John has been told that Arthur does in fact live. This fluctuating sense of truth, with Arthur alive and dead by various reports, supports Constance's sense of Arthur as a liminal entity, both present and absent. Arthur's death is not only something which Constance foresees; it is an act of adoring imagination, the only thing that will allow her to see him again. She becomes fixated on death as an abstract, becoming herself a walking *memento mori*. Her thoughts of death stray into the haptic, the olfactory, caught in paradoxes of 'odoriferous stench' and 'sound rottenness' (3.4.26). Constance relishes the physical possibilities of death inside her own head; the moment is not only one of grief but also a mental rehearsal of suicide, a vivid envisioning which struggles to negotiate death as both a sensory experience and an experience which ends the senses.

While Constance turns from negotiating her son's claim to the throne towards personal grief for a future that has passed, for others in *King John* prophecy remains a tool of politics, a way of writing what will come. Pandolf is aware that political actions dictate prophecies, rather than the other way around. As he advises Lewis, there is a great advantage if John kills Arthur because his people, so horrified by that act, will find 'meteors, prodigies, and signs / Abortives, presages, and tongues of heaven' (157–8) in the 'natural exhalation' of the sky (153). In other words, opinions are imposed upon seeming omens rather than extrapolated from them. Constance, too, who has left the stage only moments before, might then be considered to have constructed a visionary experience out of an existing emotional state, drawing her apparent certainty of the future not from supernatural knowledge but from intuition. Despite his dismissal of Constance's words as madness, Pandolf offers his own future-reading with a clear political agenda and a 'prophetic spirit' (3.4.126) that will guide Philip to the throne of England. The prophecy is little more than an aphorism which encases an obvious political reality: 'That John may stand, then Arthur must needs fall; / So be it, for it cannot be but so' (139–40). Circling itself like an ouroboros, the nature of historical drama means that all the past is inherently predicted: what will be will be because it has already been. Yet, for all its apparent inevitability, Pandolf is not fully in control of his prophecy, not realising how apt his prediction will be when Arthur *falls* to his death in the next scene.

As Pandolf's 'prophetic spirit' suggests, Constance is not exceptional in her vision; the idea of Arthur's imminent deaths spreads throughout the play as if contagious. Gina Bloom has pointed out that, although Constance is dismissed from the rest of the play, her 'vocal agency . . . seems to linger on as an agent of critique even when, perhaps especially when, her body is absent' (2005: 139). Once Constance has predicted the death of Arthur, such prophecies seem to spill from scene to scene. Prophets are, apparently, everywhere. In Act 4, Peter of Pomfret enters for some thirty lines (his entire role) to be held up by the Bastard as a 'prophet' (4.2.147) and yet is immediately imprisoned for predicting that King John will give up his crown. The vignette serves to show the danger of offering unwanted truths, and yet, within moments, Hubert (who has just escorted Peter from the stage) offers visionary reports of his own. An omen of five moons in the sky has prompted widespread future-gazing, as if the fate of Arthur is so inevitable as to be written in the night sky:

> Old men and beldams in the streets
> Do prophesy upon it dangerously.
> Young Arthur's death is common in their mouths. (4.2.186–8)

Like Constance's proleptic fear of Arthur's death, this prophecy is both false and true. Arthur will appear alive in the very next scene, only to die. In a play in which prophecy spreads through the streets and is 'common', future truth is not a scare resource, although it is a dangerous one.

Loose haired and unrestrained in her final, visionary speech, Constance offers the typical spectacle of the visionary woman. Like Cassandra, Constance unbinds her hair to reflect Arthur's own imprisonment through the spectacle of her body and its own constraints (as she has used her body to protest before, sitting motionless on the ground). Like Cassandra, she internalises the accusations of madness levied against her: she utters the word 'mad' and its variants seven times in sixteen lines, and yet, like Cassandra, she embraces her raptured state, swept towards higher truths in her state of grief. Madness is even a blessing of sensory deprivation, held against the extreme sensory awareness which Constance experiences 'too well' (3.4.59). And, madness, or rather the rage of oracular passion, might also bring with it the capacity to command attention. Constance laments her own mundanity of expression in lacking the oracle's 'thunder's mouth!' (38) which might 'shake the world' (39). Elsewhere, Shakespeare describes the 'ear-deaf'ning voice o'th'oracle, / Kin to Jove's thunder' (*Winter's Tale*, 3.1.9.10), but Constance cannot command such a sound.

After her articulation of grief, Constance is, like so many visionary women, removed from the stage. And yet, when the eventual death of Arthur plays out – although not without false starts and hesitation – it seems a resolution of Constance's insistence that 'therefore never, never / Must I behold my pretty Arthur more' (3.4.88–9). Despite resting uncomfortably between vision and intuition, Constance's words emerge as starkly realist. Unable to envisage seeing Arthur again, except as an unrecognisable spectre or formless manifestation of grief, Constance will not be swayed by social or spiritual chiding. Ignoring the seven interruptions from Pandolf and Philip which puncture her speech, Constance leaves the scene unable to find resolution. Her interior thoughts have burst forward onto the public stage; now, retreating, Constance exits to grieve within. Her offstage death, announced by a messenger in 4.2, is due to 'frenzy', if rumour can be believed (4.2.122). If true, even her madness has something of prophecy about it, as she once wished for madness herself: 'I am not mad; I would to God I were, / For then 'tis like I should forget myself' (3.4.49). However, the madness Constance longs for does not give her the satisfaction of forgetting: it means she is forgotten. She is dismissed, dying in a frenzy which undercuts her true fears; however reasonable her grief was, it will be remembered as hysteria.

5.3 Conclusion

Those who see sooth-dreams, Epistemon insists in *Daemonology*, have 'not been sharply enough examined' (1597: 75). Such claims demand scepticism and scrutiny, and this is certainly what they receive in the first tetralogy and in *King John*. Both Margaret and Constance speak warnings and curses to powerful men (indeed, to multiple rising and falling kings) and both are consequently accused of madness and witchcraft. Both women comment on and predict the political fate of those around them, taking on a choral role within their tragic world. Both women operate not only as warnings to men, serving as an onstage reminder of the dangers associated with claiming the throne, but also as accountants of loss, tallying the royal dead. They are, as the Duchess of York puts it, an 'abstract' of the past, summarising the deaths which have happened and, because of this knowledge, imagining the deaths which will come. The sooth visions of Margaret and Constance, in which they meditate on and wish for death and at moments seem to see spectres of the living, are possible because of what they have experienced. These instances of hyper-imagination are not solely a way of expressing inner turmoil: they are a rational response to a lifetime of violence.

For all their similarities, including their propensity for curses, Margaret and Constance are a demonstration of different responses to a weakened position. Whereas, at least earlier in the tetralogy, Margaret is often a successful petitionary and political player (working, for instance, to bring down Eleanor, Duchess of Gloucester), Constance is never a successful advocate, not least because she is fashioned both visually and verbally as a madwoman: full of women's fears, not future truths. Whereas Margaret wills Richard's death, and that death occurs, Constance wills her son's survival and is disappointed. Yet, both women ultimately take the same position, sitting on the ground, refusing to move in a world that allows no space for them. There is a moment of stability for both Margaret and Constance, but they must inevitably rise and face more death, moving as their own sooth-dreams, their own living ghosts, through plays that are forgetting them.

6 Conclusion: Looking Back

In the summer of 2012, standing outside in the Old College Quad in Edinburgh, I saw Teatr Biuro Podrozy's *Macbeth: Who Is That Bloodied Man?* I watched as three witches moved through the standing crowd on stilts. From a distance, the figures appeared to walk across the tops of the audience's heads, moving with precision despite the gauzy white veils covering their eyes. The closer the witches drew, tottering at an uncanny height, the more difficult they were to see in full. The planes of vision were destabilised, with no angle of sight satisfactory. I recall the sight of bodies moving above bodies: stacked and surging around me. I have looked back on this strange, hallucinatory experience many times in the decade since. The witches, subject to an audience's gaze and yet able to look quite literally above our earth-bound heads, were able to see with unmatched perspective, and, at the same time, required perspective to see. To see the witches in their entirety, and not just from below, one would have to stand apart, at the periphery of the yard. Visionary women, too, stand both apart and above, but, for all that, are able to see more clearly. This is not, however, an argument in praise of peripheral space. Shakespeare's visionary women are relegated to the periphery, only to be given a moment of revelation for which they inevitably pay.

Available to the visionary only, and impossible to prove, the vision becomes a concentrated example of the many sensory experiences and private traumas to which women are often compelled to stand as witness, both in Shakespeare and, of course, offstage. Yet, visionary women are treated as ill and unbalanced for having access to those visions. Shakespeare's visionary women emerge from their experiences with empty hands, able to articulate their experiences but unable to prove them. The vision is then a double-edged encounter with the truth, opening up central questions of witnessing and testimony before an audience, who are themselves cast in the role of dream-readers or even, in the cases of Katherine and Joan, as co-visionaries. Visions are then at once dismissed and, at the same time, wrenched from the rhetorical control of the women who experience and explain them and circulated as shared property. The vision becomes a malleable substance to be passed amongst interpreters, all of whom can draw different subjective meaning from its abstract imagery and in this way claim a kind of ownership over another's sensory experience. Yet, the blame for such visions and their warnings still lies with the visionary woman.

The visionary scene – the intercessory woman pleading with a powerful man based on the promises or threats of a vision – is played out again and again in Shakespeare, each time with slightly different circumstances which open the vision to different kinds of scrutiny. It is also, to afford due power to the many articulate female characters discussed here, an opportunity for shows of rhetorical force and political intervention, in which women, perhaps strengthened by the perceived support of a higher power, feel able and compelled to speak out. In acting as witness to some future truth, women show themselves to be astute and intuitive political players, able to see the outcomes of a tragedy that those around them do not yet understand. Yet, these charged moments of intercession in which women speak the truth do not cohere into the lesson that women's thoughts and intuitions on politics should be believed. Taking Margaret's primary visionary role as playing out in *Richard III*, only one of the eight women in these sections speaks in the final act of her play, unless her role in that act is to die. Many, like Calphurnia, disappear far sooner. They are written out, exiled, and executed: to attest to the truth ultimately proves fatal. No matter how many times this visionary scene is staged in Shakespeare, nothing seems to change.

The one surviving visionary, the final girl of this horrific pattern, is Cassandra, who lingers until the fifth act, and exits (alive) of her own volition. Cassandra admits defeat and leaves the stage with a warning couplet that sounds like a curse: 'Hector, I take my leave. / Thou dost thyself and all our Troy deceive' (92–3). The subtle agency she claims in this use of the collective pronoun ('our Troy') reaffirms Cassandra as a royal princess of Troy. The play, of course, proves her warnings true in its final scene, but not as audiences familiar with the *Iliad* might expect. For all its insistence on fatality, on prophecy which must play out in a certain way, the play ends with the brutal death of Hector, in unchivalrous circumstances not laid out by epic precedent. Here, the story goes awry, and audiences who, like visionaries, know well what should happen next, are shocked as Hector is murdered by Achilles's men and not by Achilles himself. Cassandra lives to be proved right, but in this she is an exception. Shakespeare's visionary women see the truth and suffer for it; they are feared for their capacity to think in the future tense. After all, the vision can only be proved true in retrospect and visionary women rarely last long enough to look back.

References

Artemidorus (1606). trans. Anonymous. *The judgement, or exposition of dreams*. London: R. Braddock for William Jones.

Barish, J. (1984). Madness, Hallucination, and Sleepwalking. In D. Rosen and A. Porter, eds., *Verdi's Macbeth: A Sourcebook*. Cambridge: Cambridge University Press, pp. 149–55.

Bevington, D. M., ed. (1998). *Troilus and Cressida*. Walton-on-Thames: Nelson.

Biernoff, S. (2002). *Sight and Embodiment in the Middle Ages*. Basingstoke: Palgrave.

Bloom, G. (2005). 'Words Made of Breath': Gender and Vocal Agency in *King John*. *Shakespeare Studies* 33, 125–55.

Bortolotti, L., R. Gunn, and E. Sullivan-Bissett. (2016). What Makes a Belief Delusional? In I. Mac Carthy, K. Sellevold, and O. Smith, eds., *Cognitive Confusions: Dreams, Delusions and Illusions in Early Modern Culture*. Cambridge: Legenda, MHRA, pp. 37–52.

Browne, T. (1642). *Religio Medici*. London: Andrew Crooke.
  (1991). On Dreams. In J. Gross, ed., *The Oxford Book of Essays*. Oxford: Oxford University Press, pp. 17–20.

Burns, E., ed. (2001). *King Henry VI, Part 1*. London: Arden Shakespeare, Thomson Learning.

Burton, R. (1621). *The anatomy of melancholy what it is*. Oxford: John Lichfield and James Short, for Henry Cripps.

Callaghan, D. (1992). Wicked Women in *Macbeth*: A Study of Power, Ideology, and the Production of Motherhood. In M. A. Di Cesare, ed., *Reconsidering the Renaissance: Papers from the Twenty-First Annual Conference*. Binghamton: *Center for Medieval and Early Renaissance Studies*, pp. 355–69.

Caruth, C. (1995). *Trauma: Explorations in Memory*. Baltimore: Johns Hopkins University Press.

Chess, S., C. Gordon, and W. Fisher, eds. (2019). Early Modern Trans Studies. *Journal for Early Modern Cultural Studies* 19(4), 1–25.

Clark, S. (2007). *Vanities of the Eye: Vision in Early Modern European Culture*. Oxford: Oxford University Press.

Copeland, C., and J. Machielsen. (2013). *Angels of Light? Sanctity and the Discernment of Spirits in the Early Modern Period*. Leiden: Brill.

Daniel, S. (1604). *The true discription of a royall masque presented at hampton court, vpon sunday night, being the eight of January. 1604.* London: Edward Allde.

Dawson, L. (2020). Daggers of the Mind: Hallucinations, Mental Fixation and Trauma in Kyd's *The Spanish Tragedy* and Early Modern Psychology. In H. Powell and C. J. Saunders, eds., *Visions and Voice-Hearing in Medieval and Early Modern Contexts*. Basingstoke: Palgrave Macmillan, pp. 221–54.

de Rolley, T. M. (2016). A World within: The Devil, Delusions and Early Modern Cognition. In I. Mac Carthy, K. Sellevold, and O. Smith, eds., *Cognitive Confusions: Dreams, Delusions and Illusions in Early Modern Culture*. Cambridge: Legenda, MHRA, pp. 71–88.

Dolan, F. (1994). 'Gentlemen, I Have One Thing More to Say': Women on Scaffolds in England, 1563–1680. *Modern Philology* 92(2), 157–78.

Doyle. J. E. S. (2017). Despite What You May Have Heard, 'Believe Women' Has Never Meant 'Ignore Facts'. *Elle.* www.elle.com/culture/career-politics/a13977980/me-too-movement-false-accusations-believe-women/.

Duncan-Jones, E. E. (1961). Queen Katherine's Vision and Queen Margaret's Dream. *Notes and Queries* 8(4), 142–3.

Findlay, A. (2010). *Women in Shakespeare: A Dictionary*. London: Continuum.

Fly, R. D. (1975). Cassandra and the Language of Prophecy in *Troilus and Cressida*. *Shakespeare Quarterly* 26(2), 157–71.

Fretz, C. (2016). 'Either His Notion Weakens, or His Discernings / Are Lethargied': Sleeplessness and Waking Dreams as Tragedy in *Julius Caesar* and *King Lear*. *Etudes Epistémè* 30. https://doi.org/10.4000/episteme.1383.

Frye, S. (2016). Spectres of Female Sovereignty in Shakespeare's Plays. In V. Traub, ed., *The Oxford Handbook of Shakespeare and Embodiment: Gender, Sexuality and Race*. Oxford: Oxford University Press, pp. 112–30.

Fulbeck, W. (1587). *A booke of christian ethicks or moral philosophie containing, the true difference and opposition, of the two incompatible qualities, vertue, and voluptuousnesse*. London: Richard Jones.

Gilbert, S. M., and S. Gubar. (1979). *The Madwoman in the Attic: The Woman Writer and the Nineteenth-Century Literary Imagination*. New Haven: Yale University Press.

Gilmore, L. (2017). *Tainted Witness: Why We Doubt What Women Say about Their Lives*. New York: Columbia University Press.

Gowing, L. (1996). *Domestic Dangers: Women, Words, and Sex in Early Modern London*. Oxford: Clarendon Press.

Heywood, T. (1605). *If you know not me, you know no bodie: Or, the troubles of queene Elizabeth*. London: Thomas Purfoot for Nathaniel Butter.

 (1632). *The iron age contayning the rape of hellen: The siege of troy &c*. London: Nicholas Okes.

Hill, T. (1576). *The moste pleasuante arte of the interpretacion of dreames*. London: Thomas Marsh.

Hobday, C. (1979). Clouted Shoon and Leather Aprons: Shakespeare and the Egalitarian Tradition. *Renaissance and Modern Studies* 23(1), 63–78.

Hodgkin, K. (2000). Reasoning with Unreason: Visions, Witchcraft, and Madness in Early Modern England. In S. Clark, ed., *Languages of Witchcraft: Narrative, Ideology and Meaning in Early Modern Culture.* Basingstoke: MacMillan, pp. 217–36.

Holinshed, R. (1587). *The First and Second Volumes of Chronicles.* London: John Harison et al.

Howard, J. E., and P. Rackin. (1997). *Engendering a Nation: A Feminist Account of Shakespeare's English Histories.* London: Routledge.

Jackson, G. B. (1988). Topical Ideology: Witches, Amazons, and Shakespeare's Joan of Arc. *English Literary Renaissance* 18(1), 40–65.

James I, King of England. (1597). *Daemonologie in forme of a dialogue, divided into three books.* Edinburgh: Robert Waldegrave.

Kafantaris, M. A. (2018). Katherine of Aragon, Protestant Purity, and the Anxieties of Cultural Mixing in Shakespeare and Fletcher's *Henry VIII.* In K. Mudan Finn and V. Schutte, eds., *The Palgrave Handbook of Shakespeare's Queens.* Cham: Palgrave Macmillan, pp. 331–53.

Kemp, S. (2019). Shakespeare in Transition: Pedagogies of Transgender Justice and Performance. In H. Eklund and W. Beth Hyman, eds., *Teaching Social Justice through Shakespeare: Why Renaissance Literature Matters Now.* Edinburgh: Edinburgh University Press, pp. 36–43.

Shakespeare, W. (1999). *King Henry IV Part 2.* Ed. R. Knowles. London: Arden Shakespeare.

Lanyer, A. (1611). *Salue deus rex iudæorum.* London: Valentine Simmes for Richard Bonian.

Lees-Jeffries, H. (2013). *Shakespeare and Memory.* Oxford: Oxford University Press.

Lever, C. (1607). *Queene eliȝabeths teares: Or, her resolute bearing the christian crosse inflicted on her by the persecuting hands of steuen gardner bishop of Winchester.* London: Valentine Simmes for Mathew Lownes.

Levin, C. (2008). *Dreaming the English Renaissance: Politics and Desire in Court and Culture*. Basingstoke: Palgrave Macmillan.

Levin, J. (2002). Lady MacBeth and the Daemonologie of Hysteria. *English Literary History* 69(1), 21–55.

Levin, R. (1989). Women in the Renaissance Theatre Audience. *Shakespeare Quarterly* 40(2), 165–74.

Levine, N. S. (1994). The Case of Eleanor Cobham: Authorizing History in *2 Henry VI*. *Shakespeare Studies* 22(10), 104–21.

Mack, P. (1992). *Visionary Women: Ecstatic Prophecy in Seventeenth-Century England*. Berkeley: University of California Press.

Maguire, L., and Aleksandra Thostrup. (2020). 'Fearful Echoes Thunder in Mine Ears': Hearing Voices in Marlowe's *Doctor Faustus*. In H. Powell and C. J. Saunders, eds., *Visions and Voice-Hearing in Medieval and Early Modern Contexts*. Basingstoke: Palgrave Macmillan, pp. 255–80.

Minton, G. E. (2018). 'Discharging less than the tenth part of one': Performance Anxiety and/in *Troilus and Cressida*. In P. Edward Yachnin and P. Badir, eds., *Shakespeare and the Cultures of Performance*. Aldershot: Ashgate, pp. 101–19.

Nashe, T. (1594). *The terrors of the night or, A discourse of apparitions*. London: John Danter for William Jones.

Norden, J. (1586). *A mirror for the multitude, or glasse wherein maie be seene, the violence, the error, the weaknesse, and rash consent, of the multitude*. London: John Windet.

North, T. (1579). *The liues of the noble Grecians and Romanes, compared together by that graue learned philosopher and historiographer, Plutarke of Chæronea*. London: Thomas Vautroullier.

O'Hare, J. (2018). *Queen Margaret*. Cambridge: Mimeo.

Orgel, S. (1996). *Impersonations: The Performance of Gender in Shakespeare's England*. Cambridge: Cambridge University Press.

Panjwani, V. (2022). *Podcasts and Feminist Shakespeare Pedagogy*. Cambridge: Cambridge University Press.

Paxson, J. J. (2001). Shakespeare's Medieval Devils and Joan La Pucelle. In T. A. Pendleton, ed., *Henry VI: Critical Essays*. New York: Routledge, pp. 127–56.

Pernoud, R. (1964). Trans. Edward Hyams. *Joan of Arc: By Herself and Her Witnesses*. London: Macdonald.

Poulton, M. (2016). *The York Mystery Plays*. London: Nick Hern Books.

Purkiss, D. (1996). *The Witch in History: Early Modern and Twentieth-Century Representations*. London: Routledge.

Puttenham, G. (1589). *The arte of english poesie contriued into three bookes*. London: Richard Field.

Rhodes, N. (2020). Before We Sleep: *Macbeth* and the Curtain Lecture. *Shakespeare Survey 73*, 107–18.

Richards, J., and A. Thorne, eds. (2007). *Rhetoric, Women and Politics in Early Modern England*. New York: Routledge.

Roulon, N. (2016). 'Speak No More of Her': Silencing the Feminine Voice in Shakespeare's *Julius Caesar. Annali della Facoltà di Studi Umanistici dell'Università degli Studi di Milano* 69(1), 125–46.

Rush, R. M. (2021). *The Fetters of Rhyme: Liberty and Poetic Form in Early Modern England*. Princeton: Princeton University Press.

Russell, M. J. (2008). Trial by Battle in the Court of Chivalry. *The Journal of Legal History* 29(3), 335–57.

Schroeder, J. A. (2014). *Deborah's Daughters: Gender Politics and Biblical Interpretation*. New York: Oxford University Press.

Schupak, E. B. (2016). 'Lend Me Your Ears': Listening Rhetoric and Political Ideology in *Julius Caesar. Shakespeare Survey 69*, 123–33.

Schwoerer, L. G. (1998). Women's Public Political Voice in England: 1640–1740. In H. L. Smith, ed., *Women Writers and the Early*

Modern British Political Tradition. Cambridge: Cambridge University Press, pp. 56–74.

Shakespeare, W. (2000). *King Henry VI, Part 1*. Ed. E. Burns. London: Arden.

Smith, E. (2019). *This Is Shakespeare*. London: Pelican Books.

Sofer, A. (2013). *Dark Matter: Invisibility in Drama, Theater, and Performance*. Ann Arbor: University of Michigan Press.

Spiess, S. (2016). Puzzling Embodiment: Proclamation, La Pucelle, and *The First Part of Henry VI*. In V. Traub, ed., *The Oxford Handbook of Shakespeare and Embodiment: Gender, Sexuality and Race*. Oxford: Oxford University Press, pp. 93–111.

Stapleton, M. L. (1994). 'Shine It like a Comet of Revenge': Seneca, John Studley, and Shakespeare's Joan La Pucelle. *Comparative Literature Studies* 31(3), 229–50.

Starks-Estes, L. S. (2014). *Violence, Trauma, and* Virtus *in Shakespeare's Roman Poems and Plays: Transforming Ovid*. Basingstoke: Palgrave Macmillan.

Stryker, S. (2008). *Transgender History*. Berkeley: Seal Press.

Tassi, M. A. (2018). Rapture and Horror: A Phenomenology of Theatrical Invisibility in *Macbeth*. *Explorations in Renaissance Culture* 44(1), 1–26.

Thomson, L. (1999). The Meaning of 'Thunder and Lightning': Stage Directions and Audience Expectations. *Early Theatre* 2(1), 11–24.

Willis, D. (1995). *Malevolent Nurture: Witch-Hunting and Maternal Power in Early Modern England*. Ithaca: Cornell University Press.

Wright, L. J. (2021). *Henry VIII* and Henry IX: Unlived Lives and Re-written Histories. *Shakespeare Survey* 74, 283–97.

Acknowledgements

With thanks to Emma Smith and Anna Senkiw, who shared thoughts on my early drafts; to Funlola Olufunwa for her insights and performance; to my supportive and patient editor William Worthen; to both Lisa Starks and my other, anonymous reader, for all of their guidance; and to David Yates, who has been my sounding board. This research was completed with support from the Leverhulme Foundation during my Early Career Fellowship. It has been written at a time of crisis for many in UK Higher Education and while writing I have held in mind many brave colleagues who continue to protest through and beyond their teaching and research.

For Jean, who always listens.

Cambridge Elements ☰

Shakespeare Performance

W. B. Worthen
Barnard College

W. B. Worthen is Alice Brady Pels Professor in the Arts, and
Chair of the Theatre Department at Barnard College. He is also
co-chair of the Ph.D. Program in Theatre at Columbia
University, where he is Professor of English and Comparative
Literature.

Cambridge Elements ≡

Shakespeare Performance

Printed in the United States
by Baker & Taylor Publisher Services

determination and even veneration. An inflated preeminence it is the ambition of this Element to puncture.

Shakespeare's print legacy has dominated four centuries of Shakespearean reception. The reasons for this are easy to find. Criticism prefers the apparent-ness of print to the provisionality of performance. Holding the chimera of performance in mind is impossible because performance *won't stay still* (neither will print, to be fair, but like the spinning earth itself its motion isn't appreciable).

The remit of this Element is performance, however, and so it will restrict its sweeping generalizations to that arena, such as this: Shakespeare's plays were meant to be read, but the materials from which they are read – whether manuscript or print or digital – are set aside when the trumpet sounds or the curtain rises and the actor teeters onstage in buskin or slips onstage in sock. A central question this Element poses is what abides of print when it has seemingly been left behind for the couple of hours when performance pretends to make do without it.

This Element is a polemical argument that the performance determinations of print have been greatly exaggerated – from presumptions about "implied" or "embedded" stage directions, to shared lines, to the allegedly acoustic properties of lineation, and so on. For that matter, print has not just displaced our attention but abetted a critical, analytical vocabulary almost wholly derived from print. Just one thing this Element calls for, then, is a critical vocabulary less beholden to the space of the page and more tuned to temporality. For now, suffice to say that so often when we think we're talking about performance we're actually talking about print.

1.1 The Actor and the Meaningless Text

Thus far this is breathlessly announced. Yet there is a long lineage of criticism that has decried the privileging of Shakespeare's literary properties over the theatrical dimension of his plays (which inevitably prompted its own response in a call for a return to the literary dimension of the Shakespearean text, as in Lukas Erne's *Shakespeare as Literary Dramatist* of 2003). The "rediscovery" of Shakespeare's theatricality is something that – like the rise of the middle class – happens at least once a century (and

also, like the rise of the middle class, never quite arrives). Take J. L. Styan's
Shakespeare Revolution (1977) as a signal example. Such criticism strives to
surface the theatrical dimension of the printed text. Nevertheless, "stage-
centered" criticism still centers the printed text as the site of immanent
theatricality. That is, stage-centered criticism is still print-centric criticism.
Indeed, as the following hopes to demonstrate, much attention to the
performative dimension of the Shakespearean text actively works to locate
meaning *in* the text, not *on* the stage. It is, ironically, by and large "stage-
centered" work that is most culpable in the veneration of Shakespeare's
printed output.

Consider just for the moment the many, many terms employed in the
making of theater that derive from the technologies of writing, the industry
of print, and of book history: character, type, lines, casting, stereotypes,
acts, scenes, and even verse itself (the word "verse" derives from the Latin
"versus," the turn of a plow, the furrows dug into fields; "verse" is
a graphical effect, not an auditory one). Both consciously and unconsciously, print preconceives our varied approaches to the expression of
Shakespeare on stages modern and early modern. From "type" to "stereotype," from "characters" to "lines," performance has submitted to the
rationalizations of print. Yet performance is irrational, in the root sense.
Performance – especially Shakespearean performance – is bound and
determined by print.

The dominion of print over our conceptions of Shakespeare is,
from a historical perspective, odd since among the very few things
that we can say with certainty about the theater of Shakespeare is that
actors fashioned performance from handwritten materials. Quirky,
customized, even bespoke, handwritten parts rolled an actor's score
into a furled baton of individualized expression. Performances fashioned from these handwritten parts differed from performances fashioned from printed ones, because of course they did. Just as
performances fashioned from digital texts will differ from those fashioned from print. Just *how* these performances differed requires an act
of historical imagination, since those performances are unarchived,
unarchivable. In sum, the question is what abides of the form when
writing is turned into performance?

If everything we know about Shakespeare is preconceived by print, then this knowledge extends even to cultural expressions that seek to evade ink, paper, and movable type, such as acting. Yet print privileges qualities alien to acting: standardization, reproducibility, and, above all, uniformity. Print turns the artisanal art of acting into the industrial practice of duplication. Of all the things we might wish to think about "without print," then, acting is the art where we should start. For it is with acting that the master tropes of print principally occlude rather than clarify our thinking.

The early printed texts of Shakespeare also resisted standardization, of course, producing in some instances wildly variant versions. While the editorial history of Shakespeare has often honored this diversity, the long history of the Shakespearean text has resulted, today, in a remarkably homogenized *mise en page*, a homogeneity that radiates throughout the dramatic *mise en scène*. Through a series of editorial nudges – shared lines, punctuation, line numbers, choices of font, paratext, running heads, and on and on – editors unwittingly recommend but also constrain histrionic options, often mystifying modern interventions as historical intention.

To understand the impact of the design of modern critical editions of Shakespeare upon performance, Section 4 of this Element – "In through the Out Door" – suggests we stop reading texts and start looking at them. Squint just a bit until the words start to blur and the meaning comes into focus. For the editorial design of the modern Shakespearean text allows a limited range of performance options, and does so in often subtle ways. Shakespearean performance is often today only capable of what the text, and its editors, afford.

The hand of the editor may weigh heavily upon performance, but a rough definition of "theatricality" is the extent to which performance achieves escape velocity from the text. In these terms, Shakespearean performance always remains locked in textual orbit. Doomed to circle the text from which it launched and to which it will return, either safely or in flames. The particular, even unique quality of Shakespearean theatricality is, in these terms, the massive gravitational force of the text of which performance can never lose sight. It is always there, shimmering or looming – an opalescent moon or an ominous death star – but always determining the orbit of the actors who manifest its meanings.

Since we likely cannot think about Shakespeare without print, we need to shift the terms of our analysis. The printed texts of Shakespeare are necessary if we are to access Shakespeare. But let us reframe that word "access." The printed text of a play by Shakespeare is but an accessory – an accessory to the act and to the acting of Shakespeare. And it is vitally but merely an accessory to the act. The printed text of a Shakespeare play is a list of things that actors have to say in a deliberate sequence. Script is talk. Rationalized talk. And that is all it is.

To eliminate suspense, the answer to the question Janette Dillon posed in 1994 in the title of an essay in *Shakespeare Quarterly* – "Is There a Performance in This Text?" – is no. There is no performance in the text. Because the text is not enough. Let's say it in French to make it more meaningful: *Le texte ne suffit pas*. Speaking of meaningful, let's put it this way, the Shakespearean text is meaningless. "Meaningless" does not mean without meaning, however, just as stainless steel does not mean that steel will not stain. It means it will stain *less*. The Shakespearean text is mean*less* since it means far less than is often allowed. This is broadly due to the elevation, celebration, and ascension of print at the expense of performance, which can do without print, though it relies upon it. Thus what follows assembles some diverse objections to the treatment of the printed Shakespeare text as a document of meaningful performance information.

1.2 A Quartet of Queries

How might we think about Shakespeare and performance without print? How might we, in theory and in practice, emancipate our approach to Shakespearean performance without the occlusions of a medium on which performance relies but is not beholden? (And how might the word "emancipate" in the previous sentence commit this Element to an ideological project it is incapable of achieving?) Could we envision a reading strategy, a hermeneutic, even, that (re)conceptualizes a theory of relations between text and performance that emancipates the latter from the former and in so doing enfranchises both?

Again, how might we think about Shakespeare without print? We probably cannot. Or, rather, we can only *conceive* of Shakespeare without print because whatever we may mean by "Shakespeare" is already preconceived by print, which gets us back to where we started. An exercise that takes up space but gets us nowhere. (Thinking about Shakespeare without print is like thinking about the mind without the brain. The "mind" is what the brain thinks it is, but I'll withdraw this analogy lest I seem to be suggesting that the printed text of Shakespeare is to performance what the brain is to the mind. It is far more complex than that.)

Examining texts both early and modern, *Shakespeare without Print* contends that Shakespeare and performance has long been dominated by a medium alien to its expression, print, a foreign government that forecloses alternative conceptualizations and practices. This dominion is nowhere more evident than the consensus that meaning abides "in" the printed text, rather than "through" or "with" it (taken up in the following section), or even "without" it. Through a series of discrete but linked excursions into the relationship between Shakespearean print and Shakespearean performance, this Element urges – again – scholars and practitioners to challenge the pervasiveness of print, which currently overdetermines our various approaches to Shakespearean performance.

The basic argument of this Element is that both materially and metaphorically the process and products of printing have shaped and continue to shape our thinking about Shakespearean performance. So there is a special irony in a text on this topic – even a digital one, a book "without print" – when a song and dance might serve.

In brief, the sections that follow pose the following four questions:

Is there a performance in the text?
Is performance embarrassed by its text?
Does textual design afford performance?
Is there a performance in the paratext?

The answers are yes, no, yes, and possibly, though not necessarily in that order.

2 Ink Inc.

In *King Lear*, 3.7, the wounded Cornwall underestimates his injury, saying, "I have received a hurt." In his last line, before his final exit, he says to Regan, "Give me your arm."[1] Lukas Erne writes, "Stage directions as well

---

[1] The line is identical in the 1608 quarto and 1623 folio.

as implied stage directions often prompt modern editorial intervention of some kind" (Erne, 2008: 59). From the 1974 Riverside's "*Exit [led by Regan]*" to the 1997 Norton's "*Exit* CORNWALL, *led by Regan*" to the 2004 Bevington's "*Exeunt [Cornwall, supported by Regan]*," editors make the implicit explicit. Making the implicit explicit is one way to characterize editorial labor, but implied action makes editors particularly itchy and the text breaks out in a rash of explanations. In this case, editors suggest that Regan always does what Cornwall says, an argument the play does not otherwise advance.

This may seem merely a case of editorial literalism or an editorial resistance to the idea that relations between spouses can be complex. Alternatively, this may seem like editorial diligence, more to be lauded than lamented. If it does seem like diligence – even over-diligence – on the part of the editors, it will also seem like easy pickings – even over-easy pickings – on the part of this Element, which predictably would desire a less prescriptive editorial apparatus; one that would allow for the possibility that when Cornwall asks Regan, "Give me your arm," how much more interesting it would be if she doesn't.

There is nothing at all unusual about this instance. It is exemplary only in its banality. There are hundreds if not thousands of like examples that could be culled from modern editions of Shakespeare, all of which support Erne's conclusion: activities implied by the printed texts of Shakespeare's plays prompt editorial intervention. What more concerns this section is the surprising alliance between theatrical approaches to the Shakespearean text and editorial ones. For it is not just editors who break out in fits of literalism when faced with "implied stage directions." Scholars and practitioners alert to performance take their prompt from them as well:

> Shakespeare's embedded stage directions show that . . . the playwright directs the actors to use facial expressions as visual tropes that comment on the plays' text and themes. (Loomis, 2015: 116)

> [I]mplied stage directions are far more common than the explicit ones. (Steggle, 2007: ch. 3)

> They [implied/embedded stage directions] ensure that
> Shakespeare can control the actions and expressions of his
> players, precisely and permanently, for as long as his words
> are obeyed. (Slater, 1982: 33)

Whether action is alleged to be "embedded" or "implied," the proposition is
that certain words or phrases are deictic and thus prompt action ("thus"
being only the most obvious dramatic deixis). It could be pleaded – special
pleaded perhaps – that all dramatic dialogue is deictic since it is contextua-
lized by the bodies that embody it, even when those body are static.
(Stillness is a gesture too.) Such moments of "embedded" or "implied"
action – I kneel, I raise my hands, give me your arm – are perhaps super-
deictic or, better, redundant since in these instances language and body are
not just coterminous but co-incident. The actor incorporates the ink of the
text (see Figure 1).

It is more than merely perverse to suggest that the *least* interesting thing
an actor might do when they encounter an "embedded" stage direction is to

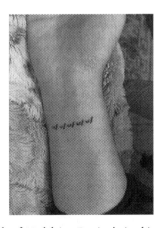

Figure 1 Photograph of Madeleine Buttitta's iambic tattoo. Photography
and permission provided by the tattooed.

"obey" it (they might just let it sleep). But there is a pervasive notion that Shakespeare embeds his theatrical intentions "in" the text, and it is among the actor's job to wake them up – even to "obey" them in Slater's terms (turning actors into the undead in the process, their zombie expressions "permanently" fixed "as long as his words are obeyed"). The extension of the logic of "implied" stage directions is that every line embeds how-to-use instructions within it. Every comma, every iamb, tells you what to do with it. This is text as super-deixis. Every word could be glossed with a "thus."

It is almost unnecessary to add that this notion exclusively concerns the Shakespearean text. No one claims that Thomas Middleton's plays are "scores," or that George Bernard Shaw's plays are "blueprints," or that those of Suzan-Lori Parks are like a "patch of code" to be "uploaded to an actor's body," as Michael Bristol says of Shakespeare's (Bristol, 2021: 57). The Shakespearean text enjoys, or suffers, a unique status, and what animates this section is this peculiar approach to the printed texts of Shakespearean plays, more precisely, the performance determinations alleged to abide in them. There is a specifically Shakespearean dramaturgy. Not just the idea that there is meaning "in" the text, but that there is a *performance* in the text, dormant, slumbering, just waiting to be shaken awake.

There is, in short, a uniquely Shakespearean performance hermeneutic. Working the same side of the street, W. B. Worthen asks, "Is Shakespeare performance a sub-subset of performance, a subset even of dramatic theatre, where special rules about the proper role of the text ... should prevail" (Worthen, 2014: 2)? To take this a step further, we might suggest that if Shakespeare is a sub-subset of performance it is a set of which it is the only one. Not a set, then, but an anomaly, even a freak. *Sui generis*, Shakespeare's printed texts are liable to a distinct critical-theatrical hermeneutic that grants those texts a power and property that are his and his alone.

This hermeneutic appears to be a neurotic symptom of a prevailing condition within the Shakespeare and performance community: a collective desire to grant an authority to dramatic texts that they cede to actors during their enactment. This transfer of power from print to performance sufficiently discomfits the interpretive community to have nagged into life an industry of analogic activity, where printed plays are relentlessly troped as forms of writing with more purchase on their enactment than playscripts. In many instances, these ascriptions of theatrical command are actually mystifications. The language of occulted intention mystifies the text so that a savior or sleuth in a robe or a deer-hunter's hat can deliver us from darkness. These analyses may look like explanations, then, but they are invocations, a summoning of orphic power for the spartan discourse of dramatic writing.

2.1 How-to-Shakespeare

In an Element of this length, examples must be indicative rather than exemplary. There are thousands of instances of the phenomenon under review here, from "embedded" or "implied" stage directions, to "shared lines," to punctuation, to verse itself. Suffice to say that while literary meaning is often imagined to inhabit the text – to reside "in" it, as Section 5 elaborates – Shakespeare's plays are uniquely alleged to contain instructions for their own performance, "how-to-use" information that should be observed, served, or even obeyed.

What expresses itself as literalism for editors manifests as figuration for Shakespeare's theatrical interpreters. For if "implied stage directions" prompt "interventions" from editors, they prompt analogies from Shakespeare's more theatrically attuned readers. Editorial literalism and theatrical figuration arrive at the same end, however: textual determinism. This idealization of the Shakespearean text as an instrument of control has produced a lush variety of tropical metaphors that mystify the relations between the Shakespearean text and Shakespearean performance. Again, the analogies search for forms of information traditionally granted more authority than dramatic scripts. Shakespeare's plays are "like" many things – scores, guides, instructions, blueprints, codes, keys, DNA, and so on – but all presuppose control and determination. However attenuated, the text intends an outcome its determinations control.

This peculiarly Shakespearean dramaturgy takes the root sense of "performance" literally. From its earliest use in a legalistic sense to its cognate "perfurnish" (now obsolete), the word "performance" signals the execution of something that precxists its enactment – a command, an agenda, an intention, a plan, or a plot. To "perform" is to proceed "by the form" (*per* = in accordance with). There is a "form" in Shakespearean "performance" and that form appears in print.

This sense of "per-formance" is dilated, for instance, by the comparison of the Shakespearean text to a blueprint: "In fact it might be said that the First Folio text is Shakespeare's blueprint for helping actors to perform his plays" (Watts, 2015: 7). The comparison articulates a central theme of all such analogies – performance is always latterly, a following-through on an already imagined, documented intention.

The opening "in fact" and the conditional "might" reveals a tenuousness, even an anxiousness, about the comparison, but give the metaphor its due. Blueprints call for creativity obscure to the novice but apparent to experts. Blueprints may detail dimensions, arrangement, and scale, for instance, but not materials or colors. To flesh out the analogy, actors bring a chromatic range to the two-tone text (the black-and-white of the printed page, the blue-and-white of the builder's plan). The relationship between draftsman and builders is collaborative. It is also creative.

Blueprints may require collaboration but they also forbid surprise. Blueprints are not provided "for helping" builders build, after all. If not followed to the letter, the roof caves in. (If an actor fails to "observe" an iamb, however, the sky is unlikely to fall.) The comparison confers upon Shakespeare the mantle of master builder, the artful architect, the deliberate designer, which exaggerates his control over the performance of his plays. Plays may be pre-scripted. That does not make them prescriptive.

To put more pressure on this metaphor than it was ever meant to bear – to lean on it until the roof caves in – the blueprint analogy offers a fantasy of control, a fantasy of precision. For the problem the blueprint emerged to answer was the intolerable deviation between imagination and realization, the quirkiness of the agents charged with duplicating the designer's intentions. Blueprints aspired to – and ultimately made way for – xerographic reproduction of the architect's original. To return to Watts's comparison of the first folio with a blueprint, we may conclude that the folio is many things but it certainly is not that. Here, the idea – again, the *ideal* – is of a stability of transfer between Shakespeare's imagination and its theatrical manifestation.

When applied to the making of early modern theater, the idea of the blueprint converts an artisanal practice into an industrial one. Blueprints (or, more technically, the cynotype process) were developed in 1842 in the midst of industrialization. They were inexpensive to produce and easy to distribute to facilitate material reproduction. By analogy, then, the folio should produce identical performances across various times and places just so long as actors understand the design. The metaphor does the ideological work such metaphors always do. It confers upon the printed text an inflated degree of performative determination. Taken to its extreme, the comparison imagines pre-fab Shakespeare.

At the same time, while it aims for accessibility, the analogy actually denies it. Blueprints are aesthetically alluring – white lines etched into a swimmy blue – but while anyone might appreciate a blueprint, it takes expertise to turn it into anything. This is a central dynamic of the figures examined here. They pull off an ambidextrous trick: on one hand they insist on the accessibility of Shakespeare's plays; on the other they insist on the technical expertise needed to perform them.

I've belabored this metaphor to establish the characteristic, even compulsory, features of such figures. Similar tropes of the play text as "instructions" reconfigure dramatic writing as forms of writing with stronger claims to regulatory agency. Consider the familiar idea of metrical language as a guide to its own enactment: "Specific detailed use of iambic pentameter affects expression of a line and this rhythm can work as Shakespeare's instructions to his actors,"[2] writes one artist. Or take the notion of the text as "guide." In the words of the Royal Shakespeare Company's former Artistic Director Gregory Doran: "Shakespeare's a guide … the answers are all in there" (Corcoran, 2018: 129). The metaphors are innocuous and therefore ideological, not least Doran's casual preposition, the "in" that pre-poses the actors' relations to the text, which in this case is a handbook that holds all the answers. Recalling the obsolete cognate "perfurnish," blueprints and instructions imagine a play as

---

[2] "Acting Shakespeare: Putting Shakespeare's Language to Practical Use," www
.discoverfineacting.com/as_notes.html.

a physical object, a tangible material thing – as though a play were a piece of flat-pack furniture with some assembly required.

To compare a playscript to a set of instructions is to deploy a metaphor in which the tenor is coupled quite closely to the vehicle. Perhaps the tenor even sits behind the wheel since the destination it drives at is one in which the playwright is in total control. To compare the Shakespearean text to a "guide" is not – to invoke Samuel Johnson on metaphysical poetry – a comparison in which heterogeneous ideas are yoked by violence together but rather one in which homogenous ones are companionably coupled. Seemingly homogenous, however, since play texts and blueprints are not fellow travelers. They are odd bedfellows.

The desire to invest the Shakespearean text with Shakespearean authority is so great as to override historical objections: Shakespeare's plays were performed without print. If the first folio *was* a blueprint, it was one the actors worked without. At the same time, it cannot be historical unawareness that lies behind these comparisons. Every scholar or artist quoted here knows that early modern actors worked from handwritten parts, not 900-page codices. These various comparisons blossom in the face of sheer fact, then. But against the desire to find a performance *in* the text, sheer fact turns into mere fact. The quaint artifactuality of handwritten parts do not stand a chance against the master tropes of print. The desire for perfurnished Shakespeare is so powerful it even trumps the allure of the handmade.

The design this blueprint actually reveals is a model of playmaking (specifically Shakespearean playmaking) with profound implications for both author and actor. In sum, the general morphology of all these tropes is one of control. Control that occurs within an industrialized process governed by the imperatives of mechanization, with its fantastic aspiration for perfect duplication.

This returns us to this book's central argument. Metaphors of the blue-*print* operate within the regime of print, a domain governed by an ethic of standardization, regulation, and rationalization – above all, an industrial process intolerant of deviation between inscription and enactment, between the word and the flesh, with its manifold and marvelous errancies.

The thicker irony here is that the notion that performance reproduces print is leveraged on an idea of reproduction borrowed from the technologies of print themselves. That is, the protocols of mechanical reproduction that govern print have been applied metaphorically to performance – and then the metaphor has evaporated, leaving only literalism behind.

This tradition of troping as mystification reaches its apogee – or nadir – in Patrick Tucker's *Secrets of Acting Shakespeare*. The book articulates "folio acting," a mystification of folio punctuation that has influenced actors in inverse proportion to the credibility of its claims. "First of all, the punctuation – the original punctuation – is I believe crucial . . .. Working from the First Folio – for the punctuation there is, I'm certain, an actor's punctuation – I insist all of it should be obeyed" (Tucker, 1994: 12). Were it not so self-conscious – "I believe . . . I am certain . . . I insist" – it would be pure charlatanism, the idea that folio punctuation, the province of typesetters, holds the keys to the kingdom, or reveals a secret that must be obeyed. What if the actual "secret" of acting Shakespeare is that there is no secret?

Patrick Tucker is not alone in insisting upon the majesty of punctuation, however. For among the various metaphysical properties ascribed to the printed texts of William Shakespeare, punctuation occupies an almost sacramental state. Judi Dench is merely typical when she commented to *The Guardian* in 2012, "If you look at the punctuation of Shakespeare and obey it, then you'll never run out of breath." Here, the immortalizing properties of Shakespearean punctuation reach its apogee: "obey" Shakespeare's punctuation and you might just live forever.

While raising, once more, the obvious historical objection that we do not have access to "the punctuation of Shakespeare," we might note the recurrence of the word "obey" that appears in Slater's, Tucker's, and Dench's quote and, indeed, across theatrical discourse on Shakespeare. Not content to "trust the text" or "serve" it, it is to be "obeyed," granting Shakespeare a more ominous sense of mastery. The most explicit manifestation of a desire to invest the text with total performative authority, "obey" reveals the true project at work here: an abject desire for servitude.

In the absence of the maker's remains, the next best thing might be his remainders. For instance, while we do not have access to "Shakespeare's punctuation," it is probable he used full stops (periods) in *Antony and*

Cleopatra, despite what Glenda Jackson told the *New York Times* in the spring of 2018 when she was playing *King Lear* at the Cort Theater, Broadway: "I've held in my hands a folio edition of 'Antony and Cleopatra.' There is only one full stop in that play. It's after the last line." She's right. There is a full stop after the last line of the play. As well as three-lines above the last line of the play. Eight lines above the last line of the play. Twelve lines above the last line of the play and on and on. There are nearly a thousand periods in *Antony and Cleopatra* alone.

What is remarkable about the claim is not its audacity, so brazenly false the *New York Times* did not fact-check it. But then why fact-check a faith-based statement? What is the more, or the most, remarkable is the willing abjection, the almost desperate claim to invest the material artifact with a sacred eminence.

The quote from Jackson ends the long feature on her, as though there were nothing left to say after the folio has been invoked. And ultimately, perhaps, that is the point, or full stop. The folio leaves nothing left to say, because it says it all. The apotheosis of Shakespearean performance would be a production that places a folio on the stage and lets it speak for itself.

2.2 Ink and Insincerity

Glenda Jackson does not believe there is only one period in *Antony and Cleopatra*. She is not making a bibliographical point about early modern punctuation. She is just providing good copy. The central irony of these abject expressions, it turns out, this outsourcing of agency from the actor to the text, is that they are insincere. It is quite obviously deviations *from* the text – actors not following "instructions" – that generate so much of the energy upon the Shakespearean stage. After all, the idea of the "blueprint" is that Shakespeare is pre-fab and that every performance would be more or less – more than less – identical, an idea no less powerful, apparently, for being so horrifying.

Even as modalities of transmission shift from writing to print and now yield to digitality – as text is minced and hashed into ones and zeros – the "insistent rhetoric of textual fidelity" (Worthen, 2014: 6) proves perdurable. One suspects though cannot prove that the insistence of this rhetoric is so insistent because those doing the insisting do not actually believe it. Even in venues where we might expect or anticipate a strong commitment to "textual fidelity" – historically allegiant theaters like the Globe or Blackfriars – meaning is made through deviations and digressions "from" the text, even *counter* to the text. In few, the rhetoric of textual fidelity is as insistent as it is insincere.

Another way to put this is that practitioners rarely practice what they preach. A signal curiosity of this form of prescriptive analysis is, then, that no one seems to believe it. It is a rhetoric, a mode, a heuristic that invests the text with performative determinations that practitioners are quite happy to ignore – and audiences quite happy to have them ignore – in practice. Astonishing actors both, neither Dench nor Jackson are noticeably punctilious in their performances of Shakespeare. They are not the Strunk and White of the Shakespearean stage. If an "embedded" stage direction or piece of "Shakespeare's punctuation" is more honored in the breach than in the observance, then it's all to the good, since the breach is where the art is.

The question that remains, baldly put, is if practitioners do not practice what they preach, why do they continue to preach it? What, in short, is actually at stake in these expressions, these critical forms of wishful thinking? Perhaps the eagerness to invest the text with performance determination is born of a recognition that even the most slavishly "faithful" theatricalizations of Shakespeare overmaster the text. Bodies always precede and supersede the text onstage. And so the various tropes, figures, and schemes attempt to re-invest the text's authority, to repair the ruptures blown into the text by performance. The various figurative investitures are, in these terms, acts of obeisance, a sacrifice and apology for the commission of theater.

As well as an excuse to do it again. Giving "Shakespeare's punctuation" its due is a way of paying him back. And paying it forward for the next time you disobey him. The tropes and schemes of mastery and control may be insincere, then, but they are no less deeply felt.

This section has peeled back the metaphysics of these metaphors to argue for the thinness of determination. Ultimately, the only determination of the text is sequence. (The rhetoric of drama is always paratactical.) As various metaphors sprout, the suspicion also blooms that their array is inversely proportionate to an uncomfortable fact: a script might just be a list of things for actors to say in a deliberate sequence. And that is all it is.

We are left to ask what deficit these ideas emerge to fill, what desire do they express? It is, I argue, the deficiency, even the insufficiency, of the text. What if a script is just and only that? Radically incomplete, gappy, thin, and underdetermined. A list of talking. What if this is all there is? A list of things for actors to say in a peculiar order. If we have to analogize the Shakespearean text, perhaps its shimmering surface appears, at first glance, to promise depths beyond depths but, when touched, turns out to be a mirror. And mirrors have nothing to hide.

This makes plain that the figurative enterprise is not in fact a system of explanation. It is a theology, a theology of the exemplary individual. These tropes do not describe something that is immanently there, they invest it with something that isn't: control, intention, determination. But perhaps, in the end, "theology" is the wrong word, or perhaps it is what Baudrillard calls "negative theology." This "apophatic" theology defines God not by what "he" is but by what he is not (Baudrillard, 2007: 187). The text is "like" a blueprint (i.e. not a blueprint). It is "like" a score (i.e. not a score). There is no identity, only identification. No meaning, only metaphors. No maker, only our desire to meet him.

3 Embarrassing Performance

3.1 Oedipus Text

Performance disguises the writing that enables it. And so among all the stuff the stage hides from the audience (water bottles, dormant costumes, thunder sheets, musical instruments, inert properties, loitering actors), textual materials – and not just the script – must remain hidden. The embarrassing fact is that actors depend on scripts, and so performance works hard to hide its embarrassment by keeping writing off the stage.

This no doubt seems crashingly obvious. Of course actors do not bring their scripts onstage. But things are sometimes so obvious that they keep us from asking why, when actors *do* bring scripts onstage, it so violates theatrical convention that we no longer call it a play. We call it a staged reading. (We do not, by contrast, call a play a "staged remembering.") It is the most obvious of ironies that the text – putative origin of performative determination – is banished from performance.

Here is another thunderingly obvious statement: most theatrical performance relies upon text. Indeed, since at least the English Renaissance the default setting for dramatic performance has been textualized drama. Performance depends upon text, and not just the script. We know this to be true, and yet the stage disguises the fact, is maybe even – as my title suggests – embarrassed by it.

This embarrassment can blister into antagonism between author and actor. Contemplating another tough day at the office, Richard Burton records in his diary on 20 March, 1969:

> I think Mr Thompson [his agent] was deeply shocked when I told him that … if I retired from acting professionally tomorrow that I would never reappear in the local amateur dramatic society for the sheer love of it. Could he not understand the indignity and boredom of having to learn the writings of another man, which nine times out of ten was indifferent, when you are 43 years old, are fairly widely read, drag yourself off to work day after day with a long lingering regretful look behind you at the book you've been interested in …? (Williams, 2012: 256)

The writing of Shakespeare is hardly "indifferent" – he's the one out of ten that Burton exempts – but Burton gets at the abiding drudgery, even servile indignity, of having to commit to memory something someone took the trouble to write down. After all, the writing is perfectly available in the form of a book, which Burton, the consummate actor, takes a long lingering look at before leaving it behind him and walking onstage.

What is a grievance for Richard Burton is a punchline for Groucho Marx:

> Almost all the successful writers I knew had been to college. Some had even graduated, and I envied them. "What was an actor?" I thought. "Nothing! Just a mouthpiece for

someone else's words. It's the writer who makes the actor good
or bad." (Marx, 1959: chapter 14)

He is kidding, I think, but Marx picks up where Burton left off. He just gives
a bit more credit to the playwright. In Groucho's view, the actor is a mechanistic
mouthpiece. Little more than a stooge, the actor is essentially a ventriloquist's
dummy. There's a man behind the curtain, and he's holding a pen.

The true crisis of this agnostic dynamic arrives when the actor is also the
author. The impossible alterity of being one and the same animates Noël
Coward, who describes the amnesia it takes to play both parts: "I always
forget, when I'm playing in my own plays, that I'm the author" (Day, 2021:
178). William Shakespeare also played in his own plays and so had to forget
himself. He possibly left a clue behind that he played Polonius. "By the mass,
I was about to say something," says the actor who knows precisely what
comes next (or, per Coward, does not). The line is a dose of self-inoculation
by an actor embarrassed at the public indecency of being exposed as an author.

What we read here is a form of Oedipus text, an embarrassment or even
antagonism that governs the relations between actors and authors. It's the
actor's job – the cliche has it – to make the dialogue sound "invented afresh,"
self-authored even or especially when the actor did not write it. This is a way
of killing the author or at least making the audience forget they exist. We
could go full Adorno here – whose fever for music never broke – and invoke
his virtuoso who "slaughters the piece of music in the name of a spellbound
community as an act of atonement" (Adorno, 2011: 66). Nothing quite so
extreme actually happens in the theater (more's the pity), but performance is
a series of antagonisms between ink and incorporation.

Sometimes embarrassment blisters into antagonism; as often it blossoms
into invention. There is almost no end to which actors will not go to
smuggle text onto the stage. To take just two idioms for extempore speech –
"winging it" and "off the cuff" – consider the ways that both rely upon the
material text they pretend to go without. The nineteenth-century actor
Anne Hartley Gilbert reminisces:

Sometimes, when we were not quite sure of ourselves, we
would take our lines along and study them between the acts,

> or during our waits. Our call would come, and we would
> tuck the parts just anywhere, usually under the slender
> wood-work of the wings; we called it "winging the
> parts." Then, if the scene were shifted, the parts would be
> whisked out of sight and reach, and there would be a great
> flutter and outcry! (*Literary Digest*, 1901: 522)

"Winging it" does not mean to fly without a net but to keep the net just out of sight.

For that matter, to speak "off the cuff" means literally the opposite of what it figuratively implies, as immortalized by Charlie Chaplin in *Modern Times* (check it out on YouTube – I'll wait right here) A performer might scribble their text on the removable cuffs once affixed to men's shirts. To speak "off the cuff" discloses the "prompt" smuggled in im*prompt*u and ultimately reveals that actors are handcuffed by the authors who put words in their mouths.

Moss Hart's marvelous account of his theatrical origins, *Act One*, parrots Burton and Marx on authorship: "I wanted, of course, to be an actor. It never occurred to me that these godlike creatures did not themselves make up the words that flowed so effortlessly and magnificently from their lips. I think I believed they created a play as they went along" (Hart, 1959: 29). Turning playwright brought these gods back down to earth for Hart, and he gives voice to the author's exasperation when he adds, "More than once, sitting in the audience at a play of mine, I have heard the lady behind me exclaim, 'The clever things actors say! Aren't they wonderful.' And I have been tempted to say, 'Not that wonderful, madame!'" Which is probably something like what Laius muttered when he first laid eyes on Oedipus.

Like Coward and Shakespeare, Hart worked both sides of the aisle, so knew how to wing it. Describing his time at summer camp working for the theatrical "impresario" Eddie, Hart recalls that

> if Eddie switched plays in the middle of the week the entire
> staff would have to heave to and help repaint the scenery, to
> say nothing of the fact that ingenious ways had to be devised
> to distribute small slips of paper with key speeches typed on

> them among the props and furniture so that we could have
> a glance at them occasionally and know what, if anything,
> we were going to say next. It was somewhat easier to
> arrange this if the plays called for an exterior set, for the
> slips could be pinned on the backs of bushes or even pasted
> unobtrusively on the top of a stone wall or fence. In the
> interiors, Eddie's wizardry at devising bits of business that
> allowed us to walk to a spot that held a piece of paper
> concealed from the audiences view, and that seemed part
> and parcel of the rightful movement of the play, was unpar-
> alleled. (Hart, 1959: 146)

What's the worst that can happen if your slip is showing? Why go to such
lengths to conceal them among the gimcrack? What harm comes if the
audience catches a glimpse of the text, the accessory to the act/ing? *Pace*
Hart, no audience member believes that actors invent dialogue on the spot
(it's the most insincere story in Hart's otherwise sincere book). Playwrights
get their name on the front of the program, after all.

Ultimately, any attempt to smuggle text onstage ends up capitulating to
the terms and conditions of the drama. James Stoddart recalls at time that
Edward Southern played Othello and "was imperfect in the words; in the last
scene he had a prompter concealed under Desdemona's bed" (Stoddart, 1902:
95). In addition to cueing the obvious joke ("Prompter? I hardly know her!"),
Southern's attempt to conceal the fact he was "imperfect" paraphrases act five
of *Othello*. Hiding the prompter under Desdemona's bed reveals Othello's
worst fears. The end has been written. The text is the cause. Let it be hid.

3.2 The Actor's Nightmare

We might call this dynamic the "protocols of preparation." The *Oxford
English Dictionary* does not put it this way, but a play is a thing not being
done for the first time. That is, a play has been rehearsed and that rehearsal
requires, at minimum, memorizations that render the material script redundant or reduces it merely to a mnemonic tool. Performance dematerializes
the material text. As an audience, then, we expect a minimum of

preparation, and that preparation includes the memorization of the script. This is a baseline assumption about attending a play. It is, in these terms, the opposite of improv. And our expectations are precisely the opposite. If you happened to stumble upon some improv and did not know they were making it up you would think it was the worst play ever written.[3]

Consider the case of *The Actor's Nightmare*. The name of a funny play by Christopher Durant, the 1991 drama was inspired by the well-known dream that many people in professional and amateur theater have, that they must perform in a play that they have never rehearsed and for which they know none of the lines. In the play, "George" is an accountant who wanders onto an empty stage, uncertain how he got there. The stage manager informs him that he is the understudy and is "on" in just a few minutes. He's pushed onstage dressed as Hamlet and finds himself opposite a character from Coward's *Private Lives*. George improvises some lines, but then the actor leaves, and on comes Hamlet. George is then left alone and must improvise his own Shakespearean soliloquy. On it goes, through pastiches of *Endgame* and *Waiting for Godot* before George faces the ax as Sir Thomas More in Robert Bolt's *A Man for All Seasons*.

The play is very funny but relies upon a certain base line presumption of theatrical performance. An actor must not carry a script onstage. In other words, what would wake George from his nightmare is a script. But if an actor carries a script onstage, they are arguably no longer an actor, or at least, as mentioned above, they are arguably no longer in a play. Being an actor in a play means being "off book." But as the actor's nightmare reveals, not having the book – or not having had the chance to convert writing into memory for automatic recall – produces genuine embarrassment, even the stuff of nightmares.

To consider the "protocols of preparation" again, compare theatrical performance to an academic conference. Sometimes even delivered from a stage, academic papers are a performance event. But few scholars would dream of coming before an audience without their text, or their paper, as the idiom "give a paper" discloses. Nor would the audience expect them to. In fact, if a scholar shows up without their text, they are not prepared. If an

---

[3] I'm indebted for this idea to the actor and teacher Thadd McQuade, who offers it in a more profane, and funnier, version.

actor shows up *with* their text, they are not prepared. Different location, same sort of physical disposition of audience and presenter. Very different sort of protocol of preparation and therefore expectation.

(We might object that an academic certainly could have memorized a lecture, and I suppose that's true. But were they to do so I suspect we would find it to be an ultimately distracting display of unnecessary work. They would have prepared, but would have prepared the wrong thing, in the wrong way. The time they lavished on memorizing their paper would have been better spent writing their paper.)

This brings us back to what an audience assumes an actor has done prior to the play almost as a contractual matter. There are a number of theatrical terms for forgetting one's lines: drying, dropping a line, going up on a line. And there are number of ways of breaking character – laughing, tripping, dropping a property, and so on – but not knowing one's lines is not a break in character but a breach of contract. The contract is between audience and actor and dictates that the actor will have memorized their lines and will be able to deliver them with effortless mastery.

This suggests that one of the things we go to the theater to see is virtuosic displays of memorization. The theater is a kind of memory circus where we see feats of great technical expertise performed by people with prodigious memories. (Actors often field this question from friends and families: "how did you memorize all those lines?" This is not actually a question but a generous expression of wonder at an actor's technical prowess.) Any remnant or semblance of onstage text ruptures our pleasure in the technical display of memory arts.

To repeat the central thesis here: theaters work to hide text wherever possible because the appearance of text onstage would break not character, and certainly not the illusion of the fiction, but the contract between actor and audience and the protocols of preparation.

3.3 *Waste Paper*

To extend this theme about the agonistic relationship between text and performance, we might think about the ways that the theater both consumes and produces text. We might, fancifully, imagine the theater as a kind of manufacturing center. It takes in writing as its raw material and fabricates fictions. But it also produces a mess of textual waste whose utility is exhausted at the end of performance. Like a cigarette, performance extinguishes itself in the act of its expression, leaving only trash behind.

This metaphor points up the particular paradox that I'm interested in exploring: in theaters modern and early modern, text may be found just about everywhere, everywhere except the stage. Consider the Blackfriars Playhouse in Staunton, Virginia, the home of the American Shakespeare Center. As a theater with some historical allegiance to early modern practice but very much beholden to modern theatrical protocols, it provides a useful locale to center this study.

Immediately on the other side of the upstage wall is not – you'd be forgiven for thinking – the English Renaissance but a typical modern backstage area, though much abbreviated (Figure 2). It includes a lot of things, but, most pertinently here, the back of the wall is lacquered with writing. This wall is, quite literally, the interface between text and performance.

Just backstage, secreted from the audience's vision, there are music cues (Figure 3), costume-change cues (Figure 4), and sound cues (Figure 5). There are prop lists, there are doubling charts, there are schedules, lists, letters, an enormous array of documents. By the end of every season, the backstage wall is absolutely plastered with text, and the actors have to take it all down before they begin wall-papering it with the next season's textual system. What that suggests is that these documents are necessary but embarrassing. Let them be hid.

It is first evident that these documents are as much part of "the play" as the script that contains the dialogue. It is also clear from the placement of this material that this text be should be invisible to the audience at all cost since it would otherwise disrupt the presumption of script-less, paper-less, unprompted, invented performance.

Since the Blackfriars pledges allegiance to history, we might add an historical aside. These documents look like early modern theatrical documents. To draw an irresponsible analogy with the past, these backstage documents are difficult to interpret even now. Imagine a theater historian 400 years in the future attempting to decipher them, trying to figure out

Figure 2 The *frons scena* of the Blackfriars Playhouse, American Shakespeare Center, Staunton, Virginia. By permission of the American Shakespeare Center.

why, for instance, one document reads "The Changeling Music List" and then, as its first item, writes "O Valencia" in a crude manuscript hand (Figure 6).

A responsible theater historian some 400 years from now will go to their text – or project it upon their retina – and determine that there is no song called "O Valencia" in what we call "the play." In fact, it's a 2006 song by The Decemberists, a fact that may well be lost to history (The Decembrists lost to history as well, though that's a different story).

Or consider why a document reads "Thomas Cue / Change List Henry VI Part I" (Figure 4). Again, imagine our future theater historian. They will

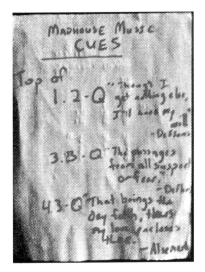

Figure 3 Music Cues for *The Changeling*, American Shakespeare Center (2009). Photo by the author. By permission of the American Shakespeare Center.

discover that there is a "Thomas" in William Shakespeare's *1HVI*, but there is no synchronicity between this list and Sir Thomas Mowbray. Maybe they will access the archives and discover that there was an actor named "Thomas Keegan" in the company at the time. That will be the more complicated once they realize that there are far more references to a "James Keegan" in the archives. The same person – 'Thomas James Keegan' – perhaps? Brothers? Father and son? (Yes.) Such documents could potentially baffle a theater historian. On one hand, then, these modern theatrical documents remind us that theatrical documents are always local, they always combine elements from "the play" – the list of words spoken by the actors – with elements of the particular immediate needs of the actors. Such documents combine the author's longhand with the actor's shorthand.

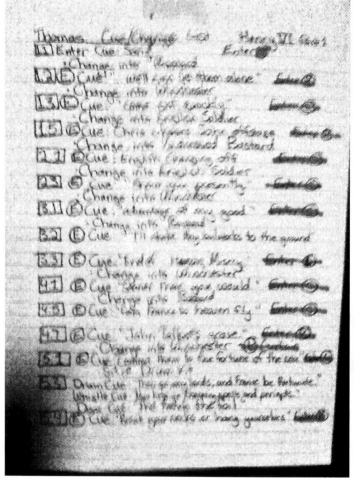

Figure 4 Costume-change cues for *1 Henry VI*, American Shakespeare Center (2009). Photo by the author. By permission of the American Shakespeare Center.

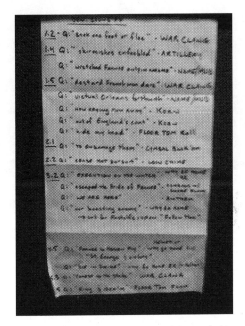

Figure 5 Sound cues for *1 Henry VI*, American Shakespeare Center (2009). Photo by the author. By permission of the American Shakespeare Center.

Returning to the ways in which theater produces and consumes paper, these documents are just ones found immediately backstage. Downstairs at the Blackfriars, as in all theaters, the green room and the dressing room and costume shop contain yet more documents that help manage and regulate the business of playing. Rehearsal schedules, union rules, safety codes, audition notices, reviews, fan letters, menus from the very few restaurants in Staunton still open after the last ovations, and on and on. Indeed, in a very cramped space the Blackfriars has found room for several computers, printers, and copiers. The playhouse is a virtual scriptorium. In sum, quite apart from documents that contain the words that the players intend to

Figure 6 List of pre-show and interlude music for *The Changeling*, American Shakespeare Center (2009). Photo by the author. By permission of the American Shakespeare Company.

speak, contemporary performances produce and rely upon a rubble of backstage textual debris.

For that matter, as at many theaters, in the Blackfriars lobby you can buy texts of the plays being performed. You can also buy badges, buttons, stickers, and tee-shirts with quotes from the plays and other slogans. Both backstage and in the lobby, the autonomous playtext is fractured, broken down, repurposed, and retailed for both the purposes of performance and profit. (Another thesis you might spin out of this is that performance is always trying to overcome its own ephemerality by attaching its text – parasite like – to the automobiles and bodies of its patrons.) At the Blackfriars, and elsewhere, the stage is, quite literally, surrounded by text, yet remarkably free of it. To be perfectly accurate, the only text in the Blackfriars proper tells the audience where to sit (row letters/seat numbers) and then orders them to leave: "*EXIT*."

Speaking of textual rubble, there are those documents that contain the actual words that the actors will speak. Backstage and in the dressing rooms, one finds complete works of Shakespeare, Middleton, Jonson, and other playwrights as well as single-play texts and even individual actor's parts, containing just their own lines and their cues. This kind of text, above all, must remain off stage to maintain the illusion. Indeed, one of the things that outrages actors is when people come to the shows with texts in hand who read along with the show (it's one of the reasons theater turned off the lights in the first place; it's hard to read in the dark). Actors always get angry when people don't look at them, but there's something particularly galling to an actor about an audience member reading *Hamlet* while they are doing *Hamlet*. This is worse than an audience member simply looking at their cell phone. It is, perhaps, not just *embarrassing* but outrageous to the performer to look out into the audience and be confronted with the very text they took the trouble to memorize.

3.4 Staged Reading

So in addition to actors disguising non-dramatic documents just out of audience view, actors develop performative techniques to disguise their text, as noted at the outset. Of course, there are those many moments in plays – particularly in plays from the early modern period, a culture of epistolarity – when actors are called on to read onstage.

Letters in the plays of Shakespeare and his contemporaries normally play an expository function. They function much like the telephone in plays from the 1930s, when the maid answers the phone and, on her end of the conversation, identifies the dispositions of the various family members. Or in all of those World War II movies in which General Exposition reads the battle plans to Major Confusion. Think of *Much Ado About Nothing*, which begins with Leonato reading a letter: "I learn in this letter that Don Pedro of . . . ." You can almost hear, across the years, the audience grumble at this bit of dogeared exposition.

Onstage reading puts actors in an uncomfortable position, however. It asks them to restage the reading they did to prepare for the moment they could put the text behind them and get on with their fake lives. From the actor's standpoint, when text *is* brought onstage, it is protocol that the actor has at least seen, read, and memorized the contents of that letter, so that the enactment of reading on the stage is still nevertheless a display of memory.

There are perils for the actor who has not memorized the letter, however. Consider the anecdote recounted of Edwin Forrest:

> On one occasion, while acting "Claude Melnotte" at the old National Theatre ... he exposed the prompter, Mr. Collingbourne, in a most emphatic manner. It is perhaps necessary to apprise the reader that all letters which are read upon the stage during a performance are previously written by the prompter. By some mistake, on this occasion, the "written letter" which "Beauseant" sends to "Melnotte" in the first act got mislaid, and the servant in the piece brought on to Mr. Forrest a blank document. The tragedian opened it as usual, and instead of finding the words, "Young man, I know thy secret, etc., etc.," he found a spotless piece of foolscap. Forrest rushed up the stage furiously, and hurling the dumb missive at the servant's head, exclaimed, "Bring me a written letter!" (Forrest, 1872)

There is then the oft-told tale about a Royal Shakespeare Company production of *Henry V* years ago when Michael Redgrave reached the point when he needs to read the names of the French dead. Montjoy failed to produce the right prop, so Redgrave starting reciting the names of some of his favorite Bordeaux producers: Chateau Cheval Blanc, Mouton Rothschild, Les Ducs de Paulliac et de St. Emillion, and so on.

Unlike Redgrave, most actors and directors prefer that prop letters have the actual lines written. Others cite a desire to have the actor's eyes move across the lines. Consider the spectacle of an actor reading a letter or book on the stage. The spectacle produces a cipher of the phenomenon under examination here. I recount from personal experience a moment in the theater that may serve as a register for this phenomena. During a production of Thomas Middleton and William Rowley's *The Changeling* at the Blackfriars, the actor Sarah Fallon was playing Beatrice Johanna, the play's heroine (if that's the right word). At one point, the script calls for her to fetch a book from her husband's closet. Fallon opened the stage door, stage right, reached inside, and withdrew a book, from which she preceded to read the medicinal potion that her husband planned to use to test her virginity.

The book looked vaguely old, old enough at least to fit into the world of Jacobean tragedy, and Fallon performed the act of reading from the book. There is a spectacularly weird effect going on here, which I will describe in layers for sake of clarity even though the point is that the effect is total and simultaneous — that is, not layered whatsoever.

The first layer is that of the fictional illusion, which is that Beatrice Johanna is reading from this book for the first time ever. A book called "The Book of Experiment, Called Secrets in Nature." (There is no book, by the way, published in English called "Secrets in Nature"; it is the playwright's invention.)

Of course, at another layer, the audience knows that it is an actor reading from a prop book, which is to say that the actor is not really reading from "The Book of Experiment" (and not just because no such book exists). She is reciting lines that she has memorized from another book, a book called *The Changeling*.

I happened to be positioned in the balcony at this performance, so I could see that Fallon had taped the particular lines she was meant to "read" inside the book. They were quite clearly handwritten, in blue ink, upon some small pieces of white paper that she had taped on the page of the book to which she opened (so, yes, her slip was showing). She hid her text inside a text, which is very clever because it's the last place you'd look.

Another way to put this is that Fallon hid the lines that she had transcribed from a text of Middleton and Rowley's *The Changeling* inside a text called for by the text of Middleton and Rowley so that she could simultaneously give the illusion that she was reading from "The Book of Experiment" while trying to convince the audience that she wasn't really reading at all but had rather memorized her lines. Even though she was "actually" reading the lines just as the fiction (revert here to layer one) suggested that she was doing. This "staged reading" serves as a complicated emblem of the way the stage simultaneously relies upon but disguises the writing that is always just on the other side of the illusion.

We might think that actors would appreciate the chance to perform a bit of staged reading, to take a break from reciting and just *read* for a change. (At least Richard Burton would.) In these terms, each letter is an olive branch from author to actor, a token of appreciation to the performers who have taken the trouble to learn their lines. But quite apart from the peril of relying on a property master to supply the right letter at the right time, the danger of not memorizing a letter, list, or book is that an audience might think an actor is *really* reading, not staging reading. However "authentic" a letter or book might look, the energy of the actor is invested in exposing it as a prop.

When Kevin Kline played Hamlet in 1990, he traced the full process considered here: the textual trajectory from mnemonic, to stage reading, to property, to waste, and then to full dematerialization. As recounted by Donald McManus,

> Where Shakespeare has Hamlet enter in Act III scene ii reading a book, Kline entered actually reading a book; he didn't pretend to read a book or use a book as a premeditated prop to catch up Polonius. Yet once the dialogue began and Hamlet called Polonius a fishmonger, the book was transformed into a prop and eventually the pages were torn out, licked and pasted on Polonius's forehead. At one point Hamlet sat reading, Marcel Marceau style, in a nonexistent mime chair, while he turned the pages saying "words, words . . . words" (Brown, 2012: 122)

Quite apart from the mind-bender of a "non-existent mime chair," we might wonder how an audience knew that Kline was "actually reading a book" versus pretending to read one. The tearing of the book fulfills the logic of "Oedipus text," and the plastering of Polonius with its remnants the actor's ultimate nightmare (reversing the terms of an actor being "off book"). Finally, Kline's staged reading – Marceau-style – mocks the authorship it relies upon by performing not the actor's nightmare but their daydream. They can make do without books after all.

The fairly obvious conclusion to this section is that textual relations – embarrassing, antagonistic, sympathetic, symbiotic – are all about authority. Theater is always a barely suppressed contest between the author's pen and the actor's voice (and the director's ashtray) and the writer always loses that contest, at least during the temporal duration of the performative act. Actors hide the text so that no one gets confused about who's in charge.

Authors might lose the battle but they always win the war. Despite Kline's best efforts to dematerialize the book, to turn it into a prop, there is a distinction to be drawn between remaindered texts and ones that remain. Shakespeare's texts abide despite the actors' best efforts to make them obsolete (you can pick up a copy of *Hamlet* as you exit through the gift shop). Actors have to simultaneously remember the text and make the audience forget there ever was one. This is impossible, and so they fail. Hiding the text only draws our attention to it. (Think of the guitar-techs at concerts who crouch as they run onstage to adjust a piece of malfunctioning guitar wizardry. Their crouching only makes them more visible.) Kline's off-book performance ultimately reminds us that plays are meant to be read.

As a final instance of this notion, we can think of the tree of books that served as center-piece to the Royal Shakespeare Company's 2009 production of *The Winter's Tale* (Figure 7).

Codex comes from "*caudex*," Latin for trunk of a tree, and so a tree made of books is a splendid visual pun, like a cow made out of quarter-pounders. But it is a joke with a serious punchline. The theater has traditionally been quite antagonistic to text and usually works quite hard to disguise the writing that enables it. Because text exposes the central scandal of performance, which is that all scripted theater are staged readings by people with really good memories. In fact, *all* performances of Shakespeare or other textualized drama are staged readings. They are just staged readings by off-book actors.

Figure 7 A tree of books from David Farr's 2009 *The Winter's Tale* for the Royal Shakespeare Company (revived at Lincoln Center, 2011). By permission of the Royal Shakespeare Company.

4 In through the Out Door

4.1 The Design of Everyday Texts

Every Friday afternoon during the academic term I gather with colleagues at Taste of India, the best – and worst – Indian restaurant in Staunton, Virginia. Often early, I spend the minutes watching patrons come in through the out door. This is not their fault. At fault is bad design (Figure 8).

The doors are classic "Norman Doors," named after Don Norman, who wrote about good doors and bad ones in his influential book, *The Design of Everyday Things*. He writes in the opening pages, "The design of a door should indicate how to work it without any need for signs" (Norman, 2013: 2). Here, signs do not help, they hinder. They ensure every diner

Figure 8 "Norman Doors" at Taste of India, Staunton, Virginia. Photo by the author.

opens their meal with a fumbled entrance and closes it with a false exit. What does this have to do with the plays of William Shakespeare? Everything.

Norman introduced the idea of "affordance theory" to design, or he at least popularized it.[4] It is a clunky term for an elegant idea. Affordance theory notices that physical objects convey intrinsic "how-to-use" instructions. Balls afford rolling, handles afford pulling, and books afford opening and closing. For Norman, well-designed objects do not need instructions that tell you how to use them. Doors should speak for themselves.

Books are extremely well-designed objects. They do not say "open" on their covers because the book's physique says "open." Books "afford" opening and closing, just one more thing they have in common with

---

[4] The term was coined by James J. Gibson (1966).

doors. But that's all they do. That is, books may afford paging, or leafing, rifling and turning, but they do not afford reading. They say "open" and "shut"; turn and return; flip and skip, but they will not speak for themselves. This is because reading is not an affordance; it is an activity. The "affordance" of a book will get you to the first page but will not tell you what to do once you get there, just as a door will get you in the restaurant but won't tell you whether to order the Chicken Tikka Masala or Lamb Rogan Josh (order the Lamb Rogan Josh).

"Activity centered design" asks what the book affords once it is opened. "An activity is a collected set of tasks, but all performed together toward a common high-level goal," writes Norman (Norman, 2013: 232). In these terms we can ask: what are the activities afforded by the modern Shakespeare text? Reading, studying, writing, and more editing. (Always more editing.) Texts also activate performance – if "activate" is the right word, which is the question of this book – and theories of design allow us to ask what theatrical activities are encouraged and discouraged by our texts. What performances are enabled and disabled? What performances do the modern edited texts of the plays of William Shakespeare afford and dis-afford?

Oriented by product design, this section takes a purposefully naïve look at the Shakespearean text not as a container of semantic content but as a product of design. It imports ideas from the world of design to reframe the editorial problem in Shakespeare. If we stop reading texts and start looking at them, we can appreciate the ways that Shakespeare in print allows some performances but forbids others. The driving question of what follows is this: once the books have been closed and the curtains have been opened, what sorts of performances have our texts afforded?

4.2 The Design Problem in Shakespeare

Stefan Zweig opens his 1928 review of James Joyce's *Ulysses* with: "Instructions for use: first you'll need a solid support so you don't constantly have to hold this mammoth novel while reading it, for this tome runs to almost one and a half thousand pages and weighs like lead on your joints." Zweig says a number of amazing things about *Ulysses*. He calls it a "witches' Sabbath of the spirit, a sprawling capriccio . . . a film of psychic situations, whirling and shrieking at the speed of an express train," but he opens by pointing out that *Ulysses* is heavy (Zweig, 2020: 159). And not in the sense that Led Zeppelin's 1979 "In through the Out Door" is heavy, but in the sense that bricks are heavy.[5] Every piece of literature made by human hands needs to be held, handled, and hefted by humans and is, in the first analysis, a made thing. Books are designed to be opened and shut, like doors.

About a decade after Zweig found Joyce too heavy to handle, W. W. Greg gave a lecture at Cambridge called "The Editorial Problem in Shakespeare," which subsequently appeared in print under the same name (Greg, 1942). The phrase stuck and Greg's principles still govern much of the approach to the preparation of the Shakespearean text nearly a century later. Approaching the Shakespearean text as an "editorial problem" disguises the fact that the problem today is mainly one of design, however. Most of the "editorial problems" of Shakespeare have either been solved or have proven insoluble. Most editorial labor is thus consumed with arraying old apparatuses in newly legible ways or adding new apparatuses in hypothetically helpful ones. This is not like re-arranging the deck chairs on the Titanic. It's more like adding two exits for every entrance to ensure we get more out of the text than we put into it.

Most editions of Shakespeare today are capably, sometimes even brilliantly edited. The reasons that an edition might be less than brilliant are not often editorial ones, though. Most editions try to activate different kinds of activities, even contradictory ones: the student, the scholar, and the actor open the book toward different ends. They pursue different "high-level goals." Editors know that a text designed for one specific activity, one specific audience, will be more coherent than one designed for a range of activities and audiences. Publishers know this too but their "high-level goal" is to shift as many units as possible. Thus most editions try to be all things to all people and produce some kind of consensus by disappointing everyone.

---

[5] Not coincidentally the name of the third studio album by L7, released in 1992.

If the editorial problem of Shakespeare *is* one of design, then what is the root problem with the design of the Shakespearean text? What's at the heart of the heart of the problem? From the perspective of performance – and for the purposes of this section – "the" fundamental design problem breaks down into three: conceptual mapping, featurism, and constraints. (Because you are already thinking it, digitality will seem like the solution to all of these problems. This section will try to exit through that door. Predictably, it is locked.) These three design problems do not exhaust the design flaws with modern editions of Shakespeare but daylight the impact that textual design can have upon performance and the ways that textual design inheres to and interferes with the performance of the words entombed in our texts.

4.3 Conceptual Mapping

An example of conceptual mapping – in design terms – would be to array a row of light switches from left to right upon the wall to "map" the arrangement of the ceiling lights they illuminate. (The toggle that automatically reclines your car seat is shaped like a car seat, a conceptual map made by a literal-minded designer.) Conceptual mapping is useful because light switches afford switching but they do not convey their relationship to the lights they turn on and off. It is fair to say that this design principle is unevenly applied to the light switches of the world. You probably have a light switch in your home that, however long you have lived there, requires some real thought every time you use it. It is not your fault. The fault is bad design.

Moving to the Shakespearean text, we can think of it as a conceptual map of performance and analyze the performances it tries to switch on. Take, for instance, the serried dialogue on the page, which corresponds graphically, geo-graphically, to the temporal sequence of dramatic speech, enabling the "one-at-a-time" speaking decorum that obtains only ever on the stage. The printing of dialogue provides a widely understood conceptual map. In order to speak in order we follow the textual, conceptual map.

The setting of "shared lines" extends this conceptual map more minutely but often gets lost along the way. Let's look at an example, exemplary in its typicality (Figure 9).

This holy shrine, the gentler sin is this:
     My lips, two blushing pilgrims,[7] ready stand
          To smooth that rough touch with a tender kiss.
JULIET   Good pilgrim, you do wrong your hand too much,
     Which mannerly° devotion shows in this.
     For saints[8] have hands that pilgrims' hands do touch,
          And palm to palm is holy palmers'° kiss.
ROMEO   Have not saints lips, and holy palmers, too?
JULIET   Ay, pilgrim, lips that they must use in prayer.
ROMEO   O then, dear saint, let lips do what hands do:
     They pray; grant thou, lest faith turn to despair.
JULIET   Saints do not move, though grant for prayers' sake.[9]
ROMEO   Then move not while my prayer's effect I take.
          [He *kisses her*]
     Thus from my lips, by thine my sin is purged.
JULIET   Then have my lips the sin that they have took.
ROMEO   Sin from my lips? O trespass sweetly urged![1]
     Give me my sin again.°
          [He *kisses her*]
JULIET   You kiss by th' book.[2]

Figure 9 *Romeo and Juliet*, Arden Shakespeare (Bloomsbury, 2012). Photo by the author. By permission of Bloomsbury.

As Norman writes of conceptual mapping, "the design projects all the information . . . needed to create a good conceptual model of the system" (Norman, 2013: 72). Here, textual design projects the idea that two actors share a metrically regular line of blank verse and do so systematically. The Juliet actor completes the Romeo actor's line without disrupting the cadence of blank verse. Spatial layout maps temporal contiguity.

"Romeo" and "Juliet" also kiss at some point during their shared line according to the stage direction (another form of conceptual mapping considered below). A kiss should take a moment – I'm told – and so the impossibility of what is modeled here is quickly evident. We've reached a fork in the road and our map tells us to take both. The actors cannot kiss in the middle of a shared line. This is a Norman door, the editorial equivalent of asking us to "push" a handle.

What has gone wrong here? Design. Shared lines exemplify one root design problem with the Shakespearean text, which may be expressed by the following question: Do shared lines map a theatrical effect or record a theatrical practice? Is the modern Shakespearean text a map of a place we have already been or a place to which we have yet to go?

David Carnegie, for one, imagines that shared lines record theatrical practice. He writes in his edition of *Twelfth Night* that though the folio does not split a "shared line" between Olivia and Viola, "we have 'stepped' it to reproduce typographically what an Elizabethan actor would have done in performance . . . , which conveys to an audience an ever closer involvement with each other." The text is a record of a remote performance, though what an "Elizabethan actor would have done in performance" is more than we can know.

Still others imagine that "stepped lines" produce, not record, performance. The Royal Shakespeare Company's online resource for teachers asks, "Why does Shakespeare write shared lines for the characters at this point in the play?"[6] (Why does the Royal Shakespeare Company write "characters" here when probably they mean "actors"? Surely "characters" do not share lines since they don't know what's coming.) In any event, the assumption is that Shakespeare intentionally wrote shared lines to produce a performance, and the printed texts honor that intention. This may even be true.

Whether record or incitement – a map of a journey already completed or one we've yet to take – the editorial assumption is that a shared line of blank verse allows two actors to sustain the pace of speaking. But what happens between the end of one actor's "complete" line of blank verse and the following pentameter line? Yawning silence? What actually happens, on the page, is a hard return. But then, to repeat, so often when we think we are speaking about performance we are actually talking about print.

The most iconic instance of "shared lines" in the editorial tradition of Shakespeare appears in *Macbeth*, 2.2 (Figure 10). It is impossible to prove but hard not to conclude that editors "step" these lines because it creates a staircase for Macbeth to descend, turning the text into a kind of "shape poem" like Herbert's "Easter Wings" (Figure 11). Stepping lines about

---

[6] www.rsc.org.uk/shakespeare-learning-zone/romeo-and-juliet/language/key-terms.

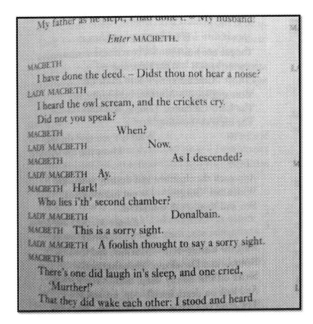

My father as he slept, I had done't. — My husband!

Enter MACBETH.

MACBETH
I have done the deed. – Didst thou not hear a noise?
LADY MACBETH
I heard the owl scream, and the crickets cry.
Did not you speak?
MACBETH   When?
LADY MACBETH   Now.
MACBETH   As I descended?
LADY MACBETH Ay.
MACBETH Hark!
Who lies i'th' second chamber?
LADY MACBETH   Donalbain.
MACBETH This is a sorry sight.
LADY MACBETH A foolish thought to say a sorry sight.
MACBETH
There's one did laugh in's sleep, and one cried,
  'Murther!'
That they did wake each other: I stood and heard

Figure 10 *Macbeth*, 2.2. *The Norton Shakespeare* (1997). Photo by the author. By permission of W. W. Norton.

steps is the kind of ingenuity that lets an editor justify knocking off early for the day.

To take a brief detour into editorial history: this typographical innovation did not exist in early modern print, though some printed dramatic texts did set "shared lines." Sometimes possibly to indicate a metrical feature; sometimes to save space. Figures 12 and 13 show two examples from *The Fair Maid of the Exchange* by Thomas Heywood (?), first printed in 1607, a play about a character tastefully named "Cripple," who is unfairly made. The first shared line achieves penta-metricality; but the second does not. "Nothing neither way," to quote Hamlet's line judge.

But as for this iconic moment of shared lines in *Macbeth*, nobody knew these lines were shared until the late eighteenth century. Not Nicholas

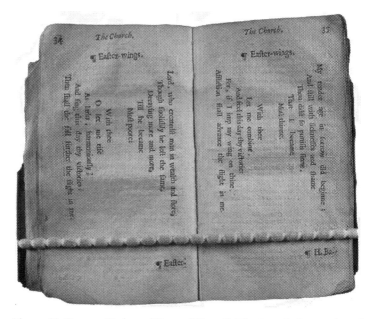

Figure 11 George Herbert, "Easter Wings," *The Temple* (T. Buck and R. Daniel, 1635.). By permission of Hathi Trust.

Rowe (1709); not Alexander Pope (1723–25); not Louis Theobald (1733); not Thomas Hammer (1744); not Samuel Johnson (1765); not Edward Capell (1767); not Edmund Malone (1790). They were too busy weaponizing the quibble to be building staircases. It was George Steevens in 1793 who first stepped these lines, and editors have taken the stairs ever since (Figure 14).[7]

---

[7] The 2016 Pelican edition of *Macbeth* does not step these lines but elsewhere uses the typographical convention of shared lines. It would be interesting to know the editor's rationale, though paratext rarely tells the reader why the editor has *not* done something.

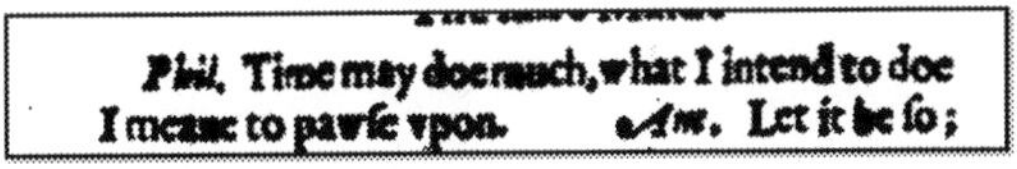

Phil. Time may doe much, what I intend to doe
I meane to pawſe vpon. *Am.* Let it be ſo;

Figure 12 A "shared line" from *The Fair Maid of the Exchange*, 1607. By permission of EEBO.

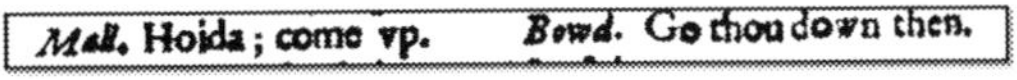

Mall. Hoida; come vp. *Bowd.* Go thou down then.

Figure 13 A "shared line" from *The Fair Maid of the Exchange*, 1607. By permission of EEBO.

416 MACBETH.

Enter MACBETH.

MACB. I have done the deed:—Didſt thou not hear a noiſe?
LADY M. I heard the owl ſcream, and the crickets cry.
Did not you ſpeak?
MACB. When?
LADY M. Now.
MACB. As I deſcended?
LADY M. Ay.
MACB. Hark!—
Who lies i'the ſecond chamber?
LADY M. Donalbain.
MACB. This is a ſorry ſight.*
[*Looking on his hands.*

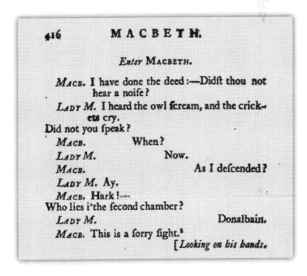

Figure 14 The Macbeth's staircase from George Steevens's *Works of William Shakespeare* (1793). By permission of Hathi Trust.

But let's close the door on the past and re-enter the present. The attempt – as the editorial instructions to the Arden Performance Editions put it – is to "make the connection visually explicit" when "the metrical connection between lines seems unambiguous" (Menzer, 2017: x). As noted, in design terms, making the connection "visually explicit" is an instance of conceptual mapping. Typographical lineation maps – or produces – an auditory effect.

Shared lines may be "visually explicit" on the page but they are usually not audibly explicit – or even apparent – in performance, unless actors collude to make them so. The irony is that when, cued by the printed text, actors *do* choose to make shared lines audibly apparent, they draw our attention to print, the medium that performance attempts to evade. And so the setting of shared lines may be an exertion by print – a land grab of sorts – to reseize its dominance.

To be sure, there are moments in the Shakespeare canon where attention is drawn to poetic form, to the way the words being uttered appear on the page. Take, once again, Romeo and Juliet's shared sonnet, where the metrical connection may be not just "unambiguous" but entirely the point (although disrupted by the "implied stage direction" of the kiss). If meticulously observed by the actors, the written form of the sonnet may be summoned for the auditors, a moment where speaking turns back into writing, even a moment where performance acknowledges its writerly dependence, becomes "meta-textual" as opposed to "meta-theatrical." This is a rarity, however; generally speaking, audiences do not notice shared lines because they do not notice un-shared ones. Lines, in performance, *don't exist*. They are purely a typographical phenomenon. Stepped lines are light switches that don't turn anything on.

Stepping shared lines can descend into confusion. Once the editor has helped Macbeth down the stairs, how do they distribute the lines that follow (see Figure 10)? Which bits go with which? How does it all add up? What do we do with the leftovers, those odd numbers? The metrical connection of these lines seems pretty ambiguous, but the text renders them visually explicit. Here, metrical fastidiousness leads to metric determinism – everything must add up to ten (though sometimes lines go up to eleven). Short lines equal shared lines except when something doesn't quite add up.

The fussiness with shared lines is abetted here (and everywhere) by line numbers. They support one another, since line numbers sustain the conforming rationale of shared lines in which everything answers to a numerical governor. The line numbers are also determined by a ten-count, always guided by a decimal logic in which – whether we tabulate lines by 5s or 10s – everyone must be rounded up to a whole number, a complete work.

Any Shakespearean who teaches modern drama will find themselves surprised to find that most plays do not come pre-counted. Line numbers may seem inevitable now – an industry standard like universal track-widths in rail-roading, though mileage may vary from edition to edition because prose is dictated by page width not line breaks. In fact line numbers did not make their first appearances until the 1863 publication of William George Clark and John Glover's edition of Shakespeare, which later became the highly influential Globe Shakespeare. In the preface to their edition, Clark and Glover write that one of their editorial objectives was "to number the lines in each scene separately, so as to facilitate reference" (Clark & Glover, 1863: ix). I will consider this further in the following section, but line numbers – designed to "facilitate reference" – are among the many tactics of information management that now accompany (or surround) the Shakespearean text.

The Norton is standard in numbering the Shakespearean text at every fifth line. This creates a sometimes exasperating scenario for students and scholars, who are familiar with the phenomenon of having to count forward or back to a line that did not pay us the courtesy of bowing to the decimal governor. This is not difficult because five is a "class-0 number" and class-0 numbers are easy to apprehend. This identification is called "subitizing," a word and idea coined by E. L. Kaufman in 1949 to refer to the process where the number of items in a set may be instantly apprehended. The human eye can apprehend that five lines fall between 5 and 10 (or 100 and 105, or 315 and 320, etc.), subitize them, and then add or subtract to solve for Shakespeare. In other words, the text tells us, *you* do the math.

Without question, line numbers are a useful indexical system for pedagogical and rehearsal practices. A way to get everybody on the same page or to at least line up. Useful, expedient certainly, but what are the implications? That the text is an operating instrument – a punch card, a time sheet, a ticker taper. Above all, the text is something we can count on.

The idea of the shared line is that there can be no hitch or glitch in a performance. The implications of this are readily apparent. Take the curious case of Shakespearean pace much circulated on the Internet: "Shakespeare is usually spoken at the rate of 1000 lines per hour so you can get a rough estimate how long each play is in performance."[8] Or, "As a rule of thumb, 1000 lines of Shakespeare's text converts to about one hour of stage time, when performed."[9] Citing such prestigious sources as "usually" or "a rule of thumb," these authoritative assertions are likely abetted – even afforded – by the design of the text as an operating system, the Shakespeare iOS.

Shared lines and line numbers are not alone in their attempt to conceptually map performance, to regulate the irregular art of acting. Take the interfering stage direction in the *Romeo and Juliet* exchange. It has to appear some*where* in the text, though it records or produces something that happens some*time* in performance. Whenever the action they describe might occur, editors have to put them some*where*. (Where do Romeo and Juliet kiss? On the lips, I think, but then, I've read a lot of fiction.) To take another example, in *Richard III* Lady Anne "spitteth" at Richard during the middle of a "shared line" in 1.2 (Figure 15).

Authorized by the early quartos of the play, which include the direction, editors insert a stage direction that – as with the case of Romeo and Juliet – disturbs the meter. She might spit at any point – even, daringly, traversing

ANNE

Where is he?

RICHARD   Here. (⟨*She*⟩ *spits at him.*) Why dost

thou spit at me?

Figure 15 Folger Shakespeare Library, *Richard III* 2004. By permission of the Folger Shakespeare Library.

---

[8] www.degolmovie.com/liveshakespeare/playlengths.htm

[9] www.stagemilk.com/length-of-shakespeare-plays/

two lines – but print is intolerant and dictates she do so in the middle or at the end of a single line. As with the example from *Romeo and Juliet*, actors cannot observe both the stage direction – either implicit or explicit – and the convention of the shared line. Whether kissing or spitting, mouths are imagined to be simultaneously engaged in speaking, osculating, and/or expectorating. Push this handle. Pull that plate. Twist the switch.[10]

In M. J. Kidnie's innovative work on the placement of stage directions, which proposes a temporal range for directed actions, she refers to stage directions as "part of the bridge that allows theatrical personnel to move from text to performance" (Kidnie & Erne, 2004: 158). Kidnie notes that text and performance are different "media," however. So if stage directions are a bridge from the text to performance they are a strange one because they lead from a place to a time, literally a bridge to nowhere. In the design terms offered here, they look like a light switch but are actually a timer.

Underlying the design problem of the Shakespeare text – the approach that conceives of the text as a "map" – is this substitution of spatial terms for temporal ones. Henri Bergson addresses this problem, where (or when) he notes, "We are compelled to borrow from space the images by which we describe what the reflective consciousness feels about time" (Bergson, 2002: 56). I was "there" we say of events, not "I was then." The attempt to equate space and time – 1,000 lines equals one hour, stage directions happen *here* not *then* – represents the more general confusion of an object with a process. The text is the former, a performance is the latter. And so the conceptual problem with conceptual mapping is the underlying idea that the text is a map and not a calendar. The former represents space; the latter represents time.

The conceptual model of the conceptual map is conceptually flawed. But so, to be fair, is the calendrical idea. The Shakespearean text is not a map. Nor is it a timekeeping device. Neither a map nor a clock, it is a list of things that actors have to say in a certain order. And it is just that.

[10] Ironically, the indisputable case of a shared line at Hotspur's death is never made "visual explicit" in print. Percy's dying line in 5.4 ("And food for –") is completed by Prince Hal: "For worms, brave Percy: fare thee well, great heart!" Both are speaking in verse, and yet this shared line does not received the shared line treatment, which is reserved for shared pentameter.

4.4 Featuritis

The page includes a lot more than things that "actors have to say."
Macbeth's staircase leads to the footnotes, for instance, the cellar where
editors keep their meanings, box upon box of stored explanations. The stairs
also descend to "featuritis," the second design problem with the modern
Shakespearean text. "Featuritis" is the "tendency to add to the number of
features of a product," often extending the number "beyond all reason."
(Norman, 2013: 262). Creeping featuritis represents the additive principle
that – designers caution – often produces diminishing returns.

The legacy of Shakespearean editing has produced a slow, steady
accretion of textual features that pile up in drifts around the dialogue.
These features often contradict one another – one signal baffles another,
producing din, not clarity, as in the instance of shared lines and stage
directions. Neither do these features speak for themselves. They do not
signal the activities they intend to enable.

A well-designed system should be resilient against failure. Non-functioning
doors may be relatively benign – or amusing to a spectator hungry for
distraction – but there are more malign scenarios. As Norman writes,

> Designers need to ensure that controls and displays for
> different purposes are significantly different from one
> another . . .. In the design of airplane cockpits, many con-
> trols are shape coded so they both look and feel different
> from one another; the throttle levers are different from the
> flap levers (which might look and feel like a wing flap),
> which are different from the landing gear control (which
> look and feel like a wheel) (Norman, 2013: 175).

A throttle that looks like a flap lever is a matter of life and death. A footnote
that looks like a gloss is not. Still, we can apply this design principle to the
Shakespearean page and observe how editors signal the difference – or not –
between a footnote and gloss as a paradigmatic instance of featuritis.

The distinction between a footnote and a gloss is indicated – if it *is*
indicated – by their locations, length, or syntax. The length of

a footnote – and their syntactical autonomy – performs a certain interpretive authority. The brevity of a gloss authorizes itself through apposition – this equals that. Footnotes borrow their form from encyclopedias, glosses from the dictionary.

The distinction between a gloss and a footnote does not map anything, however. Sometimes glosses are in the margin, footnotes are usually at the bottom of the page. That much is clear. Sometimes the font is larger or smaller but what meaningful distinction is this meant to map? They are both switches meant to turn on meaning. One is on the wall and the other's on the floor.

Footnotes and glosses do not signify how they should be used. Yes, in the introduction editors often explain the way the page is arrayed and the different interpretive functions of a gloss, a footnote, or the cryptic collation formulae shrinking at the bottom of the page. But no one reads those introductory explanations just as no one reads the terms and conditions that come with our phones. And no one should have to read those explanations. Good design should speak for itself.

Consider the following instance from 2.1. in the 2008 Norton edition of *Romeo and Juliet*, a perfect storm of bad design and editorial elaboration, which does not clarify obscurity but produces it (Figure 16).

In the Norton edition, glosses are indicated by a degree symbol, which draws attention to a marginal gloss. Such glyphs usually hover over the end of a number to indicate temperature or the proof of alcohol. In either case the superscript glyph indicates a verifiable quantum of data derived from scientific analysis. It is unusual to find them tethered to the end of a word. They suggest that the meaning of the word has been verified, or is verifiable. Borrowed from the "hard" sciences, degree signals authorize the meanings they enable by suggesting that meaning has been analyzed and quantified.

While a degree sign is a small zero, it does not signal a footnote, as do the other superscript numerals on the page. The degree symbol is a pre-footnote, in this respect, a status to which they may one day grow up, or to which they might descend. Marginal glosses are preliminary to the explanatory ambition of a footnote. There are, in sum, degrees of meaning

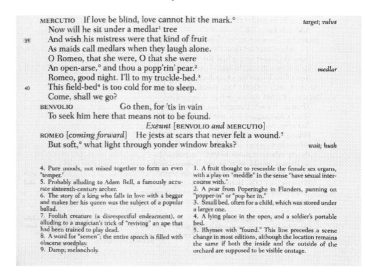

> MERCUTIO   If love be blind, love cannot hit the mark.°   *target; vulva*
>   Now will he sit under a medlar¹ tree
> 35   And wish his mistress were that kind of fruit
>   As maids call medlars when they laugh alone.
>   O Romeo, that she were, O that she were
>   An open-arse,° and thou a popp'rin' pear.²   *medlar*
>   Romeo, good night. I'll to my truckle-bed.³
> 40   This field-bed⁴ is too cold for me to sleep.
>   Come, shall we go?
> BENVOLIO   Go then, for 'tis in vain
>   To seek him here that means not to be found.
>   *Exeunt* [BENVOLIO *and* MERCUTIO]
> ROMEO [*coming forward*]   He jests at scars that never felt a wound.⁵
>   But soft,° what light through yonder window breaks?   *wait; hush*

4. Pure moods, not mixed together to form an even "temper."
5. Probably alluding to Adam Bell, a famously accurate sixteenth-century archer.
6. The story of a king who falls in love with a beggar and makes her his queen was the subject of a popular ballad.
7. Foolish creature (a disrespectful endearment), or alluding to a magician's trick of "reviving" an ape that had been trained to play dead.
8. A word for "semen"; the entire speech is filled with obscene wordplay.
9. Damp; melancholy.

1. A fruit thought to resemble the female sex organs, with a play on "meddle" in the sense "have sexual intercourse with."
2. A pear from Poperinghe in Flanders, punning on "popper-in" or "pop her in."
3. Small bed, often for a child, which was stored under a larger one.
4. A lying place in the open, and a soldier's portable bed.
5. Rhymes with "found." This line precedes a scene change in most editions, although the location remains the same if both the inside and the outside of the orchard are supposed to be visible onstage.

Figure 16 *Romeo and Juliet*, 2.1. *The Norton Shakespeare* (1997). Photo by the author. By permission of W. W. Norton.

in the paratextual features that have the text surrounded, integers on a page of text surprisingly busy with numbers.

In this instance, the degree symbols and the footnotes collaborate to explain Mercutio's innuendoes about Romeo's frustrated pursuit of Rosaline (collaborate, that is, to turn double entendres into single ones). The performer playing Mercutio may not wonder what "mark" means at the end of this opening line, but even if they did not the gloss would "reveal" that "mark" means "target; vulva" (the semi-colon implies the two words are apposite, a confusion of arrows with eros). If love is blind (or blind-folded, like Cupid), its arrows will fail to hit the bull's eye. Romeo is loosing arrows in the dark.

In the following line, Mercutio stumbles upon a footnote to the word "medlar," which may be as unfamiliar as "mark" was not. The footnote explains that a medlar "is thought" (by whom, the familiar passive construction of footnotes dares you to ask) "to resemble the female sex organs" and that there's a sexual pun on "meddle." Whatever degree of difference, thus far the paratextual features incline in one direction: Mercutio taunts Romeo for his failure to bed Rosaline and then imagines him sitting under a tree-full of vulvas lamenting the fact. So far so clear.

So far so queer, it turns out. Just four lines later Mercutio encounters the word "open-arse," which gets a degree sign not a footnote. The marginal gloss tells us an "open-arse" is a "medlar." The actor might recall that a footnote just told them that a "medlar" means "the female sex organs," possibly even the "target; vulva" of the opening "mark." The next footnote tells us that Romeo is a fruit too, a penetrating pear, but just what mark he is aiming at . . . well, we are in the dark with Cupid.

As the stevedore said to the harbor master, there's a lot to unpack here. Just what kind of sex is Mercutio talking about? The text says anal, the footnotes say vaginal (let's call the whole thing off). The text is trying to have it both ways, which may be Mercutio's point.[11] Meant to collude, gloss and footnote collide, obscuring what they mean to illuminate, reproducing the opacity they attempt to clarify or introducing a new opacity, then providing a self-nullifying explanation.

Oddly, no footnote tells the actor that "open-arse" is an editorial addition (I would say "insertion" but there are children in the audience). As is well known, the first quarto of *Romeo and Juliet* sets "*Et cetera*" after "open" while the second quarto and first folio print, "an open, or thou a Poprin Peare." Metrically speaking – sodometrically speaking – "open *Et Cetera*" is two beats too long for a pentameter line while "open, or" comes up short. In 1957 Richard Hosley introduced the now-standard reading of "open-arse," which regularizes the verse (if nothing else) and so at least makes it clear that whatever kind of sex is imagined here it will only take ten syllables.

It is a magnificent instance of editorial incoherence produced by flawed design: introduce an emendation, gloss it with a word taken from the text that itself required a footnote – a footnote that tells you it means something

---

[11] "mark; vulva."

other than what the word you introduced means. The explanatory apparatus forms a perfectly recursive feedback loop that turns signal into noise.

This may seem a local instance only, a particularly incoherent outlier, an anomaly. But the example draws attention to the competing, not colluding, apparatuses. As Norman writes, "The problem is too much information, much of it contradictory" (Norman, 2013: 183). Here the text not only does speak for itself, it talks out of both sides of its mouth. The problem is not, primarily, an interpretive one. It is, once more, a problem of design. Since in this case the gloss and footnote are at odds, how does the reader or performer adjudicate their authority? What are the power relations between a footnote and a gloss? They do not mean to, but differential placement suggests differential values – marginal glosses are marginal, footnotes are foundational.

Think back to the cockpit of that plane, with its differently shaped controls for wing flaps and landing gear. I'm not recommending that footnotes should be shaped like feet, or that glosses should shine like a fresh coat of paint (although that would be pretty). Rather, textual designers should recognize the competing claims on authority made by glosses and footnotes and consider them a product, or problem, of featuritis, those additive features that do not add up to much.

There are many many more features on the page, of course. Through-line numbers, stage directions, speech-prefixes, act/scene/line numbers, page numbers, running heads and so on. There is such a thing as subtraction through addition. It would take real courage to take features away. While we may wish for radical innovation, the most radical innovation would be to do *less* – and to do less better – to reverse the flow of editorial practice, which produces a delta of paratext that eddies around the dialogue and muddies up the meaning it tries to clarify. But, it turns out, there is a performance in the text, an editorial one. If an editor does not build a staircase for Macbeth or include collations, they run the risk of under-playing. Like an eighteenth-century actor who fails to hit their "point" – to reproduce canonical bits of stage business – if an editor does not step shared lines or gloss hard words they risk being hissed from the page. This is the legacy problem in Shakespearean editing, which inclines toward conformity. In design terms, if all else fails, standardize.

4.5 Constraints

This brings us to the final design problem considered here: constraints. In a different context, Keir Elam uses the word to describe the relations between act and inscription: "The written text constrains the performer in obvious ways – not only linguistically in determining what the actors say, and proairetically in establishing the structures of the action, but also, in varying degrees, across the range of theatrical codes by indicating movement, setting, music, and the rest" (Elam, 2002: 190). Even in this straightened account of the dramatic text, Elam probably gives it too much credit. In what ways, for instance, does a dramatic text indicate movement (or "imply" or "embed" it)? The written text no doubt "constrains" performance as much as it releases it, but the dramatic text is also constrained by its own materiality as well as by the conventions of editorial presentation, which then – it is the argument here – constrain the performer as well, in a feedback loop of self-limiting constraints.

Elam's use of the word "constraints" is useful here since he imagines the reciprocal relations between print and performance: " . . . the written text . . . is determined by . . . and indicates throughout its allegiance to the physical conditions of performance" (Elam, 2002: 191). The argument here is the opposite, however: performance is "determined by" and "indicates throughout its allegiance" to print. The truth is probably in the middle, where it so often lurks. The printed texts of Shakespeare carry a dual allegiance to performance and to print. And everywhere answer to the higher authority of editorial heritage.

In design terms, "constraints" are the set of possible operations as signified and constituted by design. The things an object allows you to do, and the limitations it places upon your activities. Consider a standard toaster, which allows you to toast a single piece of bread or even two if you're feeling peckish after building a staircase for Macbeth. If you want to toast three pieces of bread simultaneously, not consecutively, however, you'll just have to buy another toaster. In terms of constraints, you may only toast sliced bread (the greatest thing since movable type). For that matter, you may only toast bread that has been sliced to a particular width. A toaster affords certain activities, but constrains us from others.

Constraints are, then, the set of possible operations as signified and constituted by – in this case – the text's design. As Norman writes, "Natural constraints exist in the world ... that restrict the possible behavior: such things as the order in which parts can go together and the ways by which an object can be moved, picked up, or otherwise manipulated" (Norman, 2013: 76). The text can only take so much. The page can only bear so many meanings. The book has a fundamental constraint: it.

This constraints of books manifest in ways beyond page size. Books need external illumination to clarify the contrast of black ink on white paper that makes text visible in the first place. (The 2016 Pelican series of paperback editions of Shakespeare are barely visible under a forty-watt bulb since they are printed on paper a designer would call "Tuscan sunset.") When a book is too tightly bound it casts a shadow on itself. Depending upon the position of the light source, the left page shadows the right (or vice versa) so that the first word or so of every line on the right begins in darkness and ends in light (though only figuratively). Thus one constraint of printed books is that they produce their own obscurity.

Books also lack capacity for user feedback (the publisher is not going to read your marginal notes). Books are dumb, in a manner of speaking. Consider too that single-play editions of Shakespeare won't stay open, like swinging doors they close of their own volition. To hold an Arden, Folger, or Signet open with one hand you have to place a thumb upon the page, obscuring the content you are there to read. Or they require a door stop, often another, heavier book, perhaps *Ulysses*.

Constraints often produce innovation. Various Shakespeare editions have attempted ways to decompress the printed page. The Folger single-text editions place footnotes and illustrations on the left with the right reserved for dialogue. One page for meter, one page for meaning. Due to the Western reading practice, which moves from left to right, the suggestion is that interpretation *precedes* the text. The text comes pre-glossed, or at least primed with meaning.

The Arden Performance Editions flip the vector: dialogue to the left, explanations to the right. So you get what you came for the minute you step through the door. Doing so produces a retrograde reading practice, however, where the eye reflexively glances to the top of the right-hand page upon the completion of the left-hand one to discover the meaning of a word it encountered forty lines ago (or two-and-a-half minutes according to the running meter of the text).

One final feature lurks even beneath the footnotes, an instance of both creeping featuritis and a demonstration of constraints. For there is a subbasement of content that destabilizes the meaning built upon its foundation. Arguably the most inscrutable feature of an edited Shakespeare text, collation formulae – or what the late great textual scholar Tom Berger called "the band of terror" – rely upon an encoded but standardized set of typographic conventions that signal that the text is both itself and something else. There are other text(s) of the play that feature a different word, or speech prefix, or piece of punctuation at this "point" or moment in the text. If the text is a conceptual map, then collations are the foundations and the foundation is contingent.

Nothing on the page tells the reader what to do with collations – other than the arbitrary placement at the bottom of the page in type too small to read. To toggle the light-switch conceit just one last time, collations are a light switch on the wall that turns nothing on. If there is an instruction here, it is to ignore the collations altogether. You cannot read them, and even if you could you would not understand them. This reminds us of the problem of conceptual mapping while highlighting the peril of creeping featuritis. The footnotes, the glosses, and the collations bear a nonconceptual relationship to the text they aim to elucidate.

Quite apart from their contribution to creeping featuritis, collation formulae are inscrutable, legible to experts but cryptic to novices. They are the fine print of an edition, a type size reserved for the operating content – the terms and conditions that accompany a new product that we do not read but must accede to. Too small to read and too compressed to understand, collation formulae do magnify one thing: these various design problems converge upon a fundamental one, perhaps the decisive one, the problem of compression. The edited Shakespeare text concentrates a vast amount of explanatory information into a tiny space called "the page." Not all pages are uniform of course. A single page in the Folger text is about 5x7, a complete Norton more like 8x12. Still, there is a limit to how small the print can shrink before it becomes unintelligible. And no amount of pinching and expanding can uncompress printed texts to make the inscrutable scrutable.[12] Print is as stubbornly intractable as performance is not, as intractable as a locked door to which we've lost the key.

4.6 CODA: All That Text Affords

According to Wikipedia: "*Coda* is a compilation album by the English rock band Led Zeppelin. The album is a collection of unused tracks from various sessions during Led Zeppelin's twelve-year career. It was released on 19 November 1982, almost two years after the group had officially disbanded following the death of drummer John Bonham."

These references to Led Zeppelin add nothing to the meaning of this section. Consider them an example of featuritis, as if your Swiss army knife included a key to unknown door, or a toaster I suppose. However extraneous, this conclusion offers the obvious answer to the constraints of printed books: digitality, which affords endless expansion and limitless scrolling because it seems to escape constraints, allowing always and ever more features. In fact, digitality looks to evade territoriality altogether. Indeed, the deterritorialization of texts suggests they might evade *design* altogether. It might provide the running room – endless running room – the page constrains.[13] But if postmodernism has taught us anything, it's that nothing evades design.

After all, "online" books can only be read when their readers are connected to the Internet. Even when text is downloaded, readers require a phone, a laptop, or "tablet" (how quaint!) to read them, devices far more expensive and a fair bit more fragile than codex. (For that matter, they require power. No printed book ever powered down because the reader forgot to plug it in.) Even when the Shakespearean text has been deterritorialized or replatformed, it remains digitally chained to a digital desk in a digital library.

---

[12] See Piper, 2012.
[13] In a 1922 essay called "Spielraum," Karl Krause critiqued ornament in both language and design. "Spielraum" is usually translated as "running-room" but could more literally and pertinently here be considered "playing room."

For that matter, whatever alteration digital publishing has wreaked upon performance (and there has been and will be alteration), the shimmer of new technology cannot blind us to the fact that even "born-digital" books are beholden to residual forms. To be recognizable *as* books, digital ones must look an awful lot like their codex parents. Largely skeuomorphic, digital books have pages and page numbers, tables of contents and indices, and so on. They are still beholden to all manner of traditional forms. The fact that you can scroll through a digital book actually represents an archaic reversion to ancient custom. If digital books look like their codex kin, they also bear traces of their deep ancestry.

The deterritorializations of digitality are only apparent. It looks as though the text has given print the slip, and has been replatformed from codex to code, where it will enjoy endless expansion, infinite customization. But endless expansion and infinite features present their own problem. Where or when does a digital text stop? What is its principle of selection? What, in the digital space, is the difference between an edition and an archive? For all its limitations – *because* of its limitations – codex performs its principle of selection. A printed book contains only as much as it may contain. And then it stops. And so finite compression and endless expansion form the Scylla and Charybdis of the design problem with Shakespeare.

Speaking of and on art history, Hal Foster has asked, "What cultural epistemology might a digital reordering underwrite?" Such a "reordering" might seem to "fragment the object and dissolve its aura absolutely," which, inevitably, "only increases our demand for it" (Foster, 2002: 80). This might help explain the reification of print that, thus far, digital Shakespeare texts present. Meet the new text, same as the old text, only shinier.

This section has focused on the utility of design but design is driven by both utility and aesthetics. A different focus might appreciate the aesthetics of the contemporary Shakespeare critical edition, might appreciate, for instance, the extent to which the Arden3 is a pop-art masterpiece. But above all design imposes order on things, in order that we know what uses they afford. If we stop reading texts and start looking at them, if we squint just a little bit until the words start to blur, the meaning comes into focus. If there is no meaning "in" the text, there is meaning *on* it.

5 The Psychopathology of Everyday Texts

5.1 Show Invisibles

In despair, I googled it. Just up and asked the universe – or rather the metaverse – why WordPerfect kept inserting extra spaces between my paragraphs (WordPerfect – now *there's* an optimistic name!).[14] Through a veil of tears I read about "hidden" and "invisible characters," "non-printing characters," and "tons of little characters" that control how the text appears.

For that matter, the tutorial to the word processing system "Scrivener," upon which (upon?) this book was written (book?), instructs me that "the invisible characters appear in blue." This idea has not yet impacted the design of the Shakespearean text – or other dramatic texts as far as I know. Nonspeaking characters might hold their breaths until they're blue in the typeface.

It's hard to think of a better example of a text's inability to express performance than the way it disappears nonspeaking characters. The textual idea of performance is that nonspeaking characters are invisible. Just one casual effect of this is that actors will talk about how many "lines" they have to indicate the size of their role, as though speaking were the only measurable way of being dramatic.

This might seem like another design problem of the text (see "In through the Out Door" earlier, or above, or before...). A design innovation could keep silent characters before the reader's eyes (perhaps they could stand in the margin with the glosses) to remind us that bodies always supersede the text in performance.

---

[14] The title is obviously indebted to Sigmund Freud's *The Psychopathology of Everyday Life* and only slightly less obviously to Random Cloud's (1981) "The Psychopathology of Everyday Art," and owes much to the spirit of the essay, not least Cloud's ambition "rather to excite wonder than secure agreement" (122). While this footnote is acknowledging texts it does not cite, it is also indebted to W. W. Worthen's (2005) "Prefixing the Author: Print, Plays, and Performance" in *A Companion to Shakespeare and Performance* and Anthony Dawson's (2005) "The Imaginary Text, or the Curse of the Folio" in the same volume.

I don't anticipate that this idea will prove popular. It certainly will not bring about any alteration in practice. But then, as Sigmund Freud dryly notes in *The Psychopathology of Everyday Life*, "I cannot maintain that one always makes friends of those to whom he tells the meanings of their symptomatic actions" (Freud, 1995: 104). If actors are not going to carry books onstage, the text might protest: why should I give them any more space than I have to?

Speaking of Freud, "invisible characters" also point to an invisible characteristic of the text, the putative interiority of sub-textual meaning, its unconscious, buried, occulted meaning imagined to inhere "in" the text (addressed earlier, before, above . . .). If there *is* meaning "in" the text, the paratext stands grave side, shovel in hand, ready to disinter it.

The following exploration takes its cue from Pierre Macherey's *A Theory of Literary Production* (1966) with an assist from Sebastiano Timpanaro's *The Freudian Slip: Psychoanalysis and Textual Criticism* (1976). For his part, Macherey proposed a "postulate of depth," which imagines meaning to lie hidden beneath the surface: "the work is by no means what it appears: it lurks, deceptively, *behind* its real meaning" (Machery, 2006: 24). This idea abides despite, or because of, the "systematic thinness" of the work's discourse.

Macherey's work had a major impact upon cultural materialism, but left little imprint on critical editing.[15] With the "postulate of depth" in mind, we could understand glosses and footnotes to be the manifestation, rather than the revelation, of the text's putative depth. Glosses do not reveal depth, in these terms, they produce it. The marginal mirror reflects depth upon the middle. Or, just as often, paratext reproduces the opacity it attempts to clarify or introduces a new opacity that requires its own explanation.

Timpanaro enhanced Macherey's project by exfoliating the debt textual criticism owes to "the Freudian slip," or more specifically the work of Freud in *The Psychopathology of Everyday Life*. In his *The Interpretation of Dreams*, Freud speaks of "dream-thoughts hidden behind this content" and thus

---

[15] Machery has a cameo in Peter Stallybrass and Margreta deGrazia's (1993) landmark *Shakespeare Quarterly* article "The Materiality of the Shakespearean Text," which also did not have as great an impact on critical editing as it should have.

established the relationship of "in front of" and "behind," the spatial proxemics of dream work so central to literary criticism (Freud, 1995: 172). Timpanaro concludes, "Psychoanalysis and textual critics have to a large extent studied the same phenomenon" (Timpanaro, 1985: 19), a riff on Giles Deleuze's aphorism that psychoanalysis "can be summarized as follows: whatever you say, it means something else" (Deleuze, 1973: 9). To adapt this slightly, the implication of the apparatus in a critical edition is that whatever the author says, they meant something else.

Adapting Timpanaro's and Macherey's insights, we can understand glosses and footnotes as deliberate "banalizations" of the text. The term comes from critical bibliography, where it refers to the usually unconscious substitution of a word that is roughly the same as the original but more familiar to the scribe or compositor. (Copyists operate on a principle of *lectio facilior*, whereas editors usually opt for the *lectio difficilior*.) In these adopted and adapted terms, paratext is paraphrase, a doubling of the text, the margin the center's insipid shadow, even the conscious explanation of the unconscious work. The text is dreaming but the margin is awake.

5.2 Glossalia

In his *Psychopathology* Freud writes that "[at the] back of every error is a repression," or "more accurately stated: the error conceals a falsehood, a disfigurement which is ultimately based on repressed material" (Freud, 1995: 110).[16] Glosses do not presume errancy on the author's part – that is occasionally the province of footnotes or emendations – but the unwitting effect of the margin's revelations is to confer a "disfigurement" upon the text it tries to clarify. The text is not in error, but it is obscure. Editors reprise the role of compositors and construe the ornate original as its banal double. The difference being that a scribe may banalize the original unconsciously, but the editor does so intentionally. Glosses are intentional gaffes.

---

[16] Page 104 of my copy of *The Pyschopathology* contains an error in the running head so that it reads *Sychopathology of Everyday Life*. I think accuracy is the only thing being repressed in this instance.

Think back (or earlier, or . . .) to the gloss of "mark" as "target; vulva" in the 2008 Norton edition of *Romeo and Juliet*. The gloss is a repetition, a displacement, a substitution – it proposes terms of equal value (mark = target = vulva), which strips the text of its ornament and reveals the real meaning, of which this text is a euphemism. In these terms, the apparatus is not just a mirror. It turns the text into an imperfect copy of itself. The gloss suggests that this is what Shakespeare would have written had he not been such a good writer.

I want to suggest, in a tortured analogy, that this is a bit like taking a dead deer to a taxidermist, having it stuffed, and then shooting it. The relationship between center and margins looks friendly, helpful, even consensual when it can be competitive, antagonistic, even aggressive. In the *Norton Anthology of Renaissance Drama*, the text of Middleton's *Women Beware Women* features a character called "Ward" – named after his social relationship to his Guardian, who is cleverly named "Guardiano." At one point, Ward says, "There's e'en another thing too must be kept up with a pair of battledores" (2.2.84–85). The baffling line is footnoted, and the footnote is actually a gloss that's outgrown the margin. It reads, in full: "I.e., Sex is like badminton." The "i.e." in front of "Sex is like badminton" – a rejected title for this book, lamentably – signals the equivalency of footnote to phrase. "Sex" may, or may not, be "like badminton" but "Sex is like badminton" is definitely like "There's e'en another thing too must be kept up with a pair of battledores."

This is conscious banalization. The editor has not unconsciously substituted a familiar term or phrase for an unfamiliar one ("sex is like badminton" is not, to my knowledge, idiomatic). Instead, the margin takes revenge on the center's sin of obscurity. The ambition here was to write a banal shadow text at the foot of the page that reflects upon but ends up projecting the depth of the source.

By position and convention, glosses say "i.e." or "that is" or "in other words", and repeat the text, only more inelegantly. "Interpretation is repetition," as Machery puts it (Macherey, 2006: 85), but it is also diminution since every copy is at least imperceptibly smaller than the original. As noted, footnotes are often deliberately banal, even intentionally clunky. In the same anthology, in *The Woman's Prize*, Moroso says, "My nose alone shall not be played withal" (1.4.74). The footnote gives the line the high gloss treatment, though without the "i.e.": "No one is to be allowed to play with my nose like that." What motivates such an inelegant sentence? In this case, it is tempting to see the apparatus as a vendetta against the text's obscurity, except that it is not particular obscure. Moroso doesn't want anyone playing with his nose. We anticipate a footnote that explains this as an archaic idiom but are rewarded with one that doubles a clear line with a muddled one, lending it depth it otherwise lacks. The relationship of paratext to text is that of ground to surface.

We can invoke another, more obscure bibliographical term here, this time in German to make it more terrifying: "Schlimmbesserung." Roughly translated, the term describes a "disimprovement." Glosses and footnotes disimprove the text but they do so deliberately. Such "disimprovements" suggest that editors quell at the temerity it would take to improve upon the original. Citing Scherner, Freud wrote that to "'interpret a dream' is to specify its 'meaning,' to replace it by something which takes its position" (Freud, 1995: 156). Paratext does not dare to replace the text. Instead, it displaces it through a duplication. Particularly when paratext offers paraphrase, that paraphrase strives for banality and usually achieve it. Anything better would be an affront.

If a gloss or a footnote mirrors the text it is a convex mirror not a plane one since convex mirrors produce a diminished version of the original. Along with diminution there is also conversion since the paratext converts literature to information. That is, the modern Shakespeare edition brings tactics of information management to the realm of imaginative literature. (This may in part be what produces comparisons of the Shakespearean text to guidebooks, instructional manuals, and how-to-guides; see Section 1 back then, when we were young.) Generically, paratexts are finding devices and visual tools designed to help the reader get a handle on the text. Glosses and footnotes are forms of *information*; the text is a form of *imagination*. The latter is to be interpreted, the former to be understood. An intentionally inelegant paratextual paraphrase intends to make clear the distinction between one and the other. Clunky syntax communicates the idea that no imagination went into the writing of this sentence. The lack of stylistic finesse inoculates the note against interpretation. There's no more here than meets the eye. Inverting Deleuze, whatever the footnote says, it means only what it says.

It's tempting to invoke Karl Kraus's comment on psychoanalysis and say here that the gloss is the illness that thinks it is the cure. But in the modern critical edition the margins are so central because they make the middle mean. The function of the apparatus is to validate and authorize the complexity of the dramatic text by swarming it with information. The relationship of center and margin is not just interior and exterior, then; instead, the center has become an excuse for its own explanation. The text's literary status is confirmed by the statutory necessity of its marginal explanation. The marginal apparatus is now only figuratively marginal, the center also only figuratively so.

5.3 Is There a Performance in This Paratext?

Where does this leave the actor, last seen in the margins, leaving things unsaid? The question, in bald terms, is in what position, what pre-position, does the apparatus leave the actor? The apparatus can obviously not be performed, but neither can it be wholly ignored. However "unperformable," the apparatus still conditions Shakespearean performance, is still a condition of Shakespearean performance. How do actors integrate and communicate all these informational inputs?

The ambition of paratext is to shed light on anything the text might try to hide (everything except character, which isn't in the text). In editions like the Arden, the ratio of footnotes to lines varies, which tells the reader that the footnotes are in charge. The tail of explanation is wagging the dog of meaning since the page will radically reduce dramatic writing to make space for its explanation. All the meaning has been discovered; there are no more discoverables (or they would have been included since the textual design has already announced that it is quite willing to make space for any and all discoveries with the single restriction that the page must feature at least one line of dramatic dialogue).

The open question here is the extent to which paratext controls or even delimits reading. Is it a permeable border or the bars of an iron cage? Phillipe Lejeune sees something deceptive in the paratext's peripheral presence, describing it as "a fringe of the printed text of the printed text which in reality controls one's whole reading of the text" (Lejeune, 1975: 45). Gérard Genette finds something more permissive – "More than a boundary or a sealed border, the paratext is, rather, a threshold … a zone between text and off-text, a zone not only of transition but also of transaction" (Genette, 1997: 2). Actors aspire to be off book, but the question is whether they are ever off "off-text."

There is a very real chance that paratext prompts actors to imagine that among their many tasks is the conveyance of information, stored like a charged battery in the footnotes. For, to be sure, footnotes operate differently than glosses from the performer's perspective. Footnotes do not double meaning, they displace it. After all, most footnotes are not versions of "that is" ("I.e., Sex is like badminton"). Most footnotes do not suggest that meaning is beneath the actor, but beyond them. Not "beyond" an actor's capacity to understand but beyond their capacity to communicate. Footnotes about noses and badminton are just banal. But a footnote that explains, say, early modern funeral practices reminds the actor that some meanings must remain buried.

Or what's more the point, impertinent to performance. A footnote will tell an actor that a line derives from Ephesians or Thessalonians, from Plautus or Livy. Or tell them that, "the Q press-corrector probably consulted the manuscript" (Honigmann, 1996: 4.2.78fn). Or, in a footnote to "our brains' flow," that "tears were thought to exude from the brain" (Greenblatt, 2008: 5.5.81fn). The footnote's typically passive syntax establishes its authority by invoking a ghostly consensus of the past, a past that haunts the text's meaning and taunts the performer charged with conveying it.

This is not to gainsay the interest, intelligence, or accuracy of these footnotes. They illuminate, elucidate, and assist the student, scholar, or armchair enthusiast with a wide range of contextual information and suggest avenues of further inquiry. The question, once more, is the way this information positions the actor toward performance. However informative, footnotes inform them that meaning has an origin elsewhere – either in "source" text or in a historical practice or belief. Professionally occupied with a meaning's destination in performance, the text nags at the actor with a meaning's origins. The paratext positions the actor as footmen to the text.

(To be sure, the Arden or Norton texts are student- and scholar-facing texts, whereas the Arden Performance Editions – and arguably the Signet – are designed for actors. Even in the more lightly annotated Arden Performance Editions, however, glosses, metrical, and textual information receive equal time, or equal space, since each left-hand page of dialogue has a right-hand one that mirrors its meanings back at it.)

The argument here is that paratext does not reveal meaning, it produces it, largely through the introduction of discrepancies. However accurate, however synonymous, a gloss or footnote is discrepant from the text. Thus the entire apparatus operates within a program to make the printed dialogue say something other than what it manifestly says. It suggests or even recommends to the actor that their function is to correct, reveal, or disclose displaced, discrepant, and occluded meaning – to translate fiction into information. The actor becomes a supplicant to this displacement – a double agent in the service of exegesis. If not a supplicant, then a supplement. The actor does not become the author, the actor turns into just another edition, fleshy collators of variant meanings.

As throughout, the phenomenon under consideration is largely if not exclusively a Shakespearean one. After all, what makes a modern printed text of Shakespeare recognizably "Shakespearean" is the apparatus that accompanies it, that shadows it, that produces depth through duality, a doubling that telegraphs that meaning abides elsewhere, creating the elusive elsewhereness of the Shakespearean text. The elucidation of the printed text is what makes it Shakespearean. Shakespeare is that which is elucidatable.

In fact, what a strange, hybrid thing the modern Shakespearean edition has come to be. Glosses take their form from dictionaries, turning every word of dialogue into a prospective lemma. (What is the *Shakespeare Made Easy* series other than the logical end of the highly glossed text?) Footnotes, on the other hand, are encyclopedic or even resemble medieval florilegia in convening sources and quotations from a vast array of ancillary texts. The imaginative literature centered on the page and marginal information that surrounds it share space and typeface but require different reading strategies. Information is meant to be useful and truthful, literature is not, or at least is usually the worse for answering to the claims of utility and fact.

In a state-of-the-art critical edition, then, the text comes lacquered with meaning, a palimpsest of intention and identification, of exposition and exegesis. To quote Geoff Dyer on double- or treble-exposed photographs, "As with any palimpsest . . . , it's not that an ultimate meaning lies hidden beneath the various layers; its mysterious truth *is* the combination of erosion and accumulation achieved by the layers" (Dyer, 2021: 43). To translate this idea to theatrical performance, palimpsestual texts – layered with multiple temporalities and infinite intentions – instruct the actor to say "mark," but to mean "vulva," and/or to perform both. Or perform and communicate the relations between the one and the other, past and present, obscurity and illumination, to surface the mysterious combination of "erosion and accumulation" that constitutes the modern Shakespearean text.

5.4 The Last Bradleyites

The revelation for the twenty-first century reader of *The Psychopathology of Everyday Life* or of *The Interpretation of Dreams* is their resemblance to the work of Arthur Conan Doyle. As with the Holmes tales, the ingenuity of the discovery masks the implausibility of the diagnosis.

The invocation of Arthur Conan Doyle brings up another A. C. – Andrew Cecil Bradley. Since there are no coincidences in cultural life – according to Catherine Belsey – the corresponding life spans of Arthur Conan Doyle, Sigmund Freud, A. C. Bradley, and Constantin Stanislavsky are worth a look in, particularly as pertains to the work of actors. After all, if the text is just the neurotic symptom of an unexpressed, inexpressible, or even suppressed meaning – Shaw referred to his dramatic writing as a "sane hallucination" – then from the armchair of the margin, the apparatus analyses the recumbent text, which turns the actor into the interpreter of dreams.

In addition to sharing parallel life spans, Sigmund Freud (1856–1939), Konstantin Stanislavsky (1863–1938), and A. C. Bradley (1851–1935) (and even Conan Doyle) share the distinction of having established the terms by which Shakespearean acting is still widely understood – and widely reviewed – at least in the vernacular. And this closing look at Bradley's influence aims to emphasize the congeniality of critical apparatuses to histrionic approaches to Shakespeare that above all constitute a search for invisible characters.

The idea – by now the thoroughly naturalized commonplace – that exhibiting an inner life is the principal work of the mainstream actor has a discernible historical origin and identifiable intellectual sources. To take as a single, but signal, instance, the idea appears to have begun in the late nineteenth century, as the idea of the inner life achieved a crossover from an academic into a vernacular criticism that celebrates a radical form of expressivity designed to invoke the interior. We can hear a hint of the coming method in a review of Henry Irving from 1895, when a critic dismisses as modish Irving's suggestion of an inner life:

> As in the Tubal scene of "The Merchant of Venice," Irving's
> Shylock, which is so finely effective in every other scene,
> resorts to the modern myth of "suppressed passion," so in
> "Macbeth"; the actor employs the same device in a dozen
> scenes. (November 3, 1895, *The New York Times*)

There was nothing particularly "modern" even in 1895 about suppressed passion. A philosophy of productive suppression has philosophical roots in the ancients.[17] What is "modern" to this reviewer is the suppression of passion as a theatrical device. That the anonymous critic perceives it as "modern," however, registers the sea change in the manner that actors were assessed, as the always appropriative stage raided an emerging discourse and put it to its use.[18]

---

[17] See Menzer, 2006.

[18] We have further verification of Irving's approach from a review by the play-wright Charles Rann Kennedy, who after Irving's death acquired his marked up Clarendon Press copy of *Macbeth*. Writing early in the twentieth century, Kennedy remarks that Irving's notes fall into several categories, including those that register "(a) Simple emphases of particular words" and "(b) For throwing up

That "inner life" so rapidly became the metric of actorly evaluation says much about the role of the commercial theater review in indoctrinating actors, audiences, and – in a self-fulfilling loop – other reviewers into a language of interiority, a language so familiar to us that we might fail to register how recent, pervasive, and remarkable it is.

A broader historical review than is possible here could establish a rapid "norming" of the inner life as a term of critical assessment, during which the ideas of Freud, Stanislavsky, and Bradley entered the theatrical vernacular through the vector of commercial journalism, altering and then codifying theatrical training, performance, and above all the terms of assessment of what constitutes histrionic quality.

In these terms, twenty-first century Shakespearean acting is still immanently eighteenth and early nineteenth century, since three eminent figures from the age – Freud, Bradley, and Stanislavsky – coined the terms by which we still evaluate acting, terms that are largely a form of popularized psychoanalysis. In short, what constitutes "skill" on the mainstream stage continues to be the ability, in Stanislavski's terms, to give artistic form to "the inner life of the human spirit" (Stanislavski, 1995: 14).

The arrival of "psychology" to the theatrical vocabulary is hinted at by a spectacularly unprophetic early review of A. C. Bradley's *Shakespearean Tragedy*. Writing in the *Athenaeum* in 1905, the unsigned critic presages that

> these essays of Prof. Bradley are designed for a wide public, which they appear to be well on their way to secure, and may possibly even exercise some influence upon stage production. This, however, will necessarily be faint, the anxiety of the manager-actor, who alone is in the position to mount and present a Shakespearean tragedy, being rather to furnish opportunities for histrionic accomplishment or spectacularly display than to cast any strong light upon psychology, or to

values in psychology, characterization or story." In Kennedy's evaluation, Irving attended to both pronunciation and psychological nuance, which become increasingly comfortable with one another. Folger Scrapbook B.77.1 "Macbeth"

> extract from scene and situation their final significance.
> (May 13, 1905, *The Athenaeum*)

The critic correctly predicted Bradley's popular appeal but badly under-estimated the impact his book would have on the theatrical profession. For depending upon your perspective, it is either a frustrating or a delicious irony – or both – that one of the most energetically discredited works of twentieth-century Shakespearean criticism has arguably exerted the greatest academic influence upon the performance of Shakespeare onstage over the last 100 years.

The publication of A. C. Bradley's *Shakespearean Tragedy* in 1904 has played an outsized but largely unacknowledged role in the history of Shakespeare and performance (it is another irony that this work was originally a performance – a series of lectures – but made its mark through print). There is a specific irony about Bradley's impact upon performance. It is not merely that the impact persisted in the face of the academic backlash against character criticism – an aggression produced by and productive of Bradley's massive influence, an aggression that has waned now that character criticism has, inevitably, made a comeback.

But a solid plank in the anti-Bradley platform was that Bradley read plays as though they were novels. As Kenneth Burke and others have pointed out, however, Bradley did not "read plays as novels." He wrote plays as novels. *Shakespearean Tragedy* reads, above all, like novelizations of *Hamlet*, *Macbeth*, *Lear*, and *Othello*. Reading Bradley on *Hamlet* is like reading *Hamlet*, just with better transitions. The book is not called *On Shakespearean Tragedy*, after all; it is *Shakespearean Tragedy*, the thing itself.

Nor did Bradley disdain the stage – another common misconception. There's evidence of his playgoing – including a record of his attending a Gerhart Hauptmann comedy with Bertram Russell. That must have been fun. Furthermore, in a private letter, Bradley expressed his admiration for Granville Barker's onstage work and his distaste for Beerbohm Tree's *Tempest*, positioning his theatrical taste within the *avant garde*. Nevertheless, the idea of Bradley's theatrical naïveté persists.

Above all, the specific irony here is that actors read like Bradley. But then, Bradley read like an actor who, as he put it, "had to study all the parts." He abstracts characters from the action, isolates each for monadic attention – what we might call "rehearsal" or, better, the "character study" that anticipates it. Bradley's methods, that is, are congenial to modern theater's conventional methods of preparation, which require an actor to start their work with an isolated and affective engagement with the words they are meant to say, to unearth their "character" in a private, agonistic encounter with the text and its duplicitous paratext.

Indeed, today, character continues to provide the idiom in which the plays of Shakespeare are advertised, documented, and critiqued; in sum, character often organizes the activities of the Shakespearean theatrical experience. Yet the idea that Shakespearean actors play Shakespearean characters is – like all things – an historically contingent one, part of a tradition that *Shakespearean Tragedy* culminates, epitomizes, and perpetuates in its distillation of Freud and Stanislavsky.

Bradley's bequest to actors is, above all, the development of arguments called "characters" and a method for finding the evidence for those arguments. L. C. Knights, in his famous response to Bradley, picked on this particular aspect of Bradley's approach, noting that the "detective instinct supersedes the critical." Treating the text as a source of clues, codes, or embedded information adheres to a sort of textual forensics (See "Ink Inc." above, earlier, sooner . . .). It views the text as a crime scene and so fundamentally understands it as witness to something that has already happened. This is odd, since if the text *does* contain clues, we might imagine from the actors' perspective that they are clues to a crime that hasn't happened yet.

Bradley actually played a large part in creating the phenomenon he was attempting to anatomize. Like the man who shoots a hole in the side of a barn and draws a bull's-eye around it, A. C. Bradley went looking for character, and in the process helped to produce it. Because while L. C. Knights was right about A. C. Bradley, he was wrong in ways he did not fathom: Lady Macbeth does not have any children, but she spawned a thousand footnotes and they follow her wherever she goes. Each character does have a biography. It is the entire anthology of their critical fortunes, a biography that often underscores the text in the form of footnotes, and irradiates across all attempts to embody "her."

Henrik Ibsen premiered *A Doll's House* in London in 1898. The Moscow Arts Theatre opened that same year. The *Interpretation of Dreams* was published in 1900, while A. C. Bradley released *Shakespearean Tragedy* just four years later. It's easy enough to bring texts and events together to suggest pregnant historical parallels, but the brief attempt here is to see the ways in which ideas from thinkers and writers as diverse as Sigmund Freud, A. C. Bradley, and Konstantin Stanislavsky, not to mention Henrik Ibsen have consolidated interiority as the desideratum of actors, critics, and audiences today.

And this is what connects – at last – what might feel like a closing digression with this section's opening move. The idea that there are invisible characters in the text who need to be made visible is one fomented less by the text than by its paratext. It is furthered by approaches that understand the relations between text and meaning to be one of surface and depth, of wakefulness and dreaming. The modern critical edition of Shakespeare is, in these terms, remarkably congenial to presumptions about the end of acting. In particular, the peculiar art of *Shakespearean* acting, with its obsession with character, with the Shakespearean characters' characteristic claims on interiority. Paratextual apparatus functions as the revealed interiority of the text's subconscious, aiding and abetting and even producing the sovereign subjectivity that constitutes Shakespearean character.

I have argued here that the apparatus treats the text as a repression, as symptomatic. (If the text *is* a symptom, the disease is authorship.) In most cases, rather than unearthing neuroses, paratext finds only simplicity, banalities about noses, badminton, and vulvas. Where the text *is* genuinely obscure, the ambition is often to reduce its obscurity to the level of information, which diminishes its imaginative ambition.

"All is not glossed," as Jeffrey Masten has written, and, to be sure, most dramatic writing has to speak for itself, or wait for an actor to do so (Masten, 2016: 213). But the effect of the paratext is to promote reading strategies that favor "deep" meanings over shallow ones. It has been a subtheme of this book that the Shakespearean text is meaning*less*, but print – its protocols, its practices, its forms and functions, its agents and agencies, its editors and editions – makes the meanings appear to be fully baked. The meaning is all *in there*, just waiting to delivered to an audience hungry for a meal of meaning by actors condemned to play waiters onstage as well as off. The power of print is such that it is probably too late to imagine a scenario where the ambition of the Shakespearean actor might extend beyond ushering a book onstage. They might even aspire to be the chef.

Can there be literary interpretation without Freud? What if the text is all there is? Could we embrace a superficial editorial praxis that rejects interpretation? Can we imagine a facile histrionic approach to Shakespeare that treats the dramatic text as a list of talking? The depth-perception, or perception of depth, of literary materials is hard to evade since to some extent this is what makes them "literary." Even Terry Eagleton's arresting description of Pierre Machery's approach metaphorizes and therefore metamorphoses the text: "It is as though he turns over the neatly embroidered tapestry of the text, in which there is not a thread out of place, to expose the untidy sprawl of stitches which went into its making" (Machery, 2006: x). But what if we turned over the tapestry and discovered there's nothing there? Or, better, what if we turned over the tapestry and found only tapestry. Perhaps the marvel of literature is not that it is so mysterious but that it is so obvious about it.

The Shakespearean text is neither an expression of the author's intentions nor a simple repression of ideology. It is a formal attenuation of the former and the imperfectly shaped manifestation of the latter. (Literature participates in ideological production because it has to, because it cannot do otherwise. That is why it's called "ideology.") The production of interiority that pretends to discover it does not, however, deprive the text of its expressive power. Far from it. As Freud wrote in the final lines of *The Psychopathology of Every Day Life*, psychic material "is not robbed of all capacity to express itself" when it re-manifests in aberrant forms (Freud, 1995: 146). Paratext does not deprive the Shakespearean text of its rich, complex, weird, and beautiful properties, but it does attempt to explain them. Every paratextual entry could be prefaced by "Well, actually . . . ."

"Why do I have to activate hidden characters?" an actor might ask, quoting a website designed for writers struggling with their formatting.[19]

---

[19] https://redokun.com/blog/show-hidden-characters-indesign.

Because, the site tells you, "You want to have complete control over your text." What if the text has nothing to hide? What if the text is all there is? To reprise, what if the real secret to acting Shakespeare is that there is no secret? No depth, only surface, a glittering, shimmering, opalescent surface that does not reflect. It only projects.

6 The Quirk

6.1 Linotypicality

I will end with what might seem like a perverse move. I will end by thinking about Shakespeare with print (another book might try to think about print without Shakespeare, a project well beyond the abilities of this writer). But if we must think about Shakespeare with print – and we must, or we will, despite this book's best effort – if everything we know about Shakespeare is preconceived by print, just what kind of printing are we talking about?

When it comes to performance, the tropes of print derive from the practices of industrial-scale printing, with its aspirations for standardization. It is a curiosity, but an important one, that when we think about Shakespeare *with* print, we seem to be thinking neither about letterpress printing of the early modern period nor about offset lithography – or even the digital "press" of the twentieth and twenty-first centuries. As with approaches to acting detailed in the previous section, the printing we do our thinking with remains immanently Victorian.

To be precise, much of our print-derived vocabulary dates to the late eighteenth and early nineteenth century, with the coming of industrialization to the manufacturing of books. Take Lord Stanhope's metal printing press in the early 1800s as a signal instance. Able to produce large-format books at a rapid clip, it introduced speed and scale and prompted other relevant developments, such as the stereotype process, widely used for reprinting throughout the nineteenth and early twentieth century. If "casting" imagines the bodies of actors as molten lead poured into the contours of pre-fixed characters, "stereotyping" imagines performance as a reprint, duplicative by design, intolerant of deviation.

Perhaps most critically, linotype was invented by Ottmar Mergenthaler and used to print the *New York Tribune* in 1886 before wide adoption across the industry. Linotype introduced machine efficiencies to typesetting since it effectively replaced the errant hands of compositors with an efficient process of mechanical typesetting. Linotype – "line of type" as the name suggests – set type by line not letter. Massively more efficient, the process previews our obsessions with the Shakespearean line, that unit around which various constituents of performance, interpretation, and editing gather.

Such innovations effectively cut out the middlemen and turned a circle of craft into a production line that anticipates Fordism. It was in fact Frederick Winslow Taylor who introduced the concept of the assembly line in his *Principles of Scientific Management* in 1911. Taylor urged a division of labor that transformed traditional printing houses into industrial factories. As social critics from Marx (Karl, not Groucho) to Charlie Chaplin have noted, the division of labor is one of the hallmarks of capitalism and is what separates artisanal craftsmanship from industrial manufacturing. There is both a human and product-oriented price to pay here: with the division of labor the individual need only know how to do one specific task and nothing more. The assembly-line worker requires no large-scale knowledge, no vision, no concept of the whole. As long as the worker can turn the screw or twist the widget when the piece is in front of them, that is all they need to know and do. This allows each worker to focus on perfecting a specific set of skills and can lead to increased quality or at least efficiency.

In Ford's assembly line – with a stress on *line* – the end product was literally out of site for the vast majority of the workers. Similarly alienated from the end of their labor, linotype workers hunched like monks over their keyboards, locked into a tranced relationship with their one and only job: produce lines. (The parallel is irresistible. Stephen Orgel writes, "What actors do, after all, is not perform actions but recite lines." (Orgel, 1988: 8).)

The few images we have of early modern print shops show a process that resembles Fordism, to be fair, but with an important distinction. There is a Taylorist division of labor: composing or typesetting, dabbing the ink onto the type, turning the screw at the press, redistributing type, proofing, and so on. But all of this is happening in a single room, in a single shop, a single factory, so that the products of labor are, quite literally, all around the men (usually) who produced them. This is not an assembly line, it is a circle of craft.

The point is this: when we speak casually but inaccurately about the early modern "theater industry" – which it wasn't – we unwittingly conform an artisanal craft with an industrial practice. The effect is that when we ascribe performative determinations to the Shakespearean text, when we deploy print-derived metaphors to describe performance, we risk turning actors into middlemen, which, with the approval of Ford and Taylor, we can then cut out to maximize efficiency. Preconceived not just by print but by nineteenth-century industrial-scale printing, the texts of Shakespeare become linotypical or even like the perforated rolls fed into player pianos. Ideally, the play text can perform itself without the errant and interfering flesh of actors, who have been made redundant.

6.2 The Allure of the Handmade

It is fair to confess at this late stage that metaphors of print are not entirely inapposite when we think about Shakespearean performance. If we are to think about Shakespeare with print, however, we might think about Shakespeare with the printing practices that prevailed during his lifetime, the letterpress.

Letterpress printing – an "order permeated by individuality" – offers a reasonable resemblance to the early modern craft of playmaking. The letterpress holds the "allure of the handmade" and can reframe our thinking about the early modern theater "industry" not as an industry at all, but as an artisanal practice, one permeated by errancy, pervaded by individuality, at home with variation, and hospitable to the quirk.

After all, each issue from the letterpress is a handmade original, not a copy. It does not banish but actively implies improvisation, reappraisal, adjustment, deviation, and irregularities. There is, in David Jury's words, "the unavoidable contrast and tension . . . between regulation and freedom, uniformity and divergence," which aptly describe theatrical performance though Jury is talking about printing (Jury, 2011: 20). Early modern performance was, in these analogous terms, gloriously tolerant of errancy. Idiosyncrasy was a feature, not a bug.

And yet we usually think of print as invested in the production of duplicative, reproducible, identical sameness. Ideally, a consumer should not be able to tell the first book from the last one in a press run. And to the casual eye, they do appear identical. But early printing produced diversity, not uniformity. This is due not just to the well-known practice of stop-press correction, in which errancy was literally folded into the product. Take paper as just one more ingredient in the recipe for difference that the letterpress cooked up. Made from organic materials, paper was acutely susceptible to climatic conditions. This created size variation even within single reams. It made for different absorption rates from page to page. Even variable humidity in the print shop altered the cling of ink-to-surface. Printing was an impressionable practice and therefore – like theater – hostage to a thousand contingencies, which show up on the page and on the stage.

The handmade is no guarantee of quality of course – errant and expensive, handmade objects are in many cases inferior to those made by machines. To call early modern playmaking a "handicraft" is a descriptive, not a eulogistic, adjective, though the word glows with the elegiac. For that matter, the "hands" in "handicraft" often held tools, but then for William Morris and his followers, the term "handicraft" did not exclude the use of machines. In fact Morris valued tools as extensions of, not replacements for, the human hand. Letterpress is absolutely dependent upon tools, from composing sticks and ink paddles to the printing presses themselves. But industrial metaphors such as "typecasting" and "stereotypes" actually and actively elide the printer's craft, the interpretive role that printers played in the era of the letterpress.

The attempt to resuscitate the letterpress as a metaphor for performance is probably doomed. After all, "after five hundred years of overdetermining the production and dissemination of knowledge, the printing press appears as an antiquarian object, more likely to be seen in a great museum than in publishing houses" (Gikandi, 2012: 203). Introducing the letterpress as an analogous art to early modern acting succumbs to the overdeterminations of print and converts the body of the Shakespearean actor to a machine for reproducing meaning, however errant, however imperfect. At worst, it turns the Shakespearean text into a museal object, actors as docents, and converts all theater into "museum theater" though it remains an open question whether that term is an oxymoron or a redundancy.

6.3 Art in the Age before Mechanical Reproduction

There is no art "before" mechanical reproduction. And it certainly is not the case that the art of the English Renaissance – not least theater – occurred in an age "before" mechanical reproduction. The tweak to Walter Benjamin's phrase is, however, used here to audition the idea that acting is not an art of mechanical reproduction, though the argument of this book is that we often treat it as such.

An argument can be mounted, of course, that acting *is* an art of mechanical reproduction. What else, after all, is a "twice behaved behavior" (Schechner, 1985: 36)? But acting is an art of *bio*mechanical reproduction. Acting does reproduce itself but does so through acting and other actors, not printing and the press. For instance, gestures, like texts, quite obviously do reproduce themselves. That is how they acquire legibility. That is how they become a "gesture" not a meaningless physical tic. But gestures reproduce themselves through their own technology, the imperfectly quirky machines of the imitative human form. Acting begets acting through imperfect imitation.

This book opened with the argument that the master tropes of print occlude rather than clarify our thinking about acting. It will end by offering a way of thinking about acting *without* print. First, acting does not get better. But it does get different, and changes in acting style prompt alternatives to print to understand the embodied art of performance. Memetic theory, for instance, could help theorize a model of dissemination and adaptation of gestural information as a way to understand the evolution of changes in mimetic style. Originally coined in 1976 by the geneticist Richard Dawkins, the term "meme" now appears in the *Oxford English Dictionary*, where it is defined as an "element of culture that may be considered to be passed on by non-genetic means, especially imitation." The cognitive psychologist Susan Blackmore explored the dizzying implications of the idea that gesture, behaviors, tunes, and ideas reproduce (at least metaphorically) like genes. Whenever you whistle the theme from *Star Wars*, wear a ball cap backward, or bless yourself in church, you are trafficking in memes. Or, to put it more ominously, memes are trafficking in you.

In the early modern period, "apish acting," or slavish imitation, was a frequent charge against poor playing. In the terms of memetic theory, such imitation is distasteful simply because it is not selectively imitative. Mimicry implies a phenotype (the product) that does not become genotype (the copy of the product). Following the lead of evolutionary biologists, we could argue that some aspects of acting styles – a word too small to capture gesture, posture, vocal inflections, and so on – reproduce and others do not, not because they are "fitter" but because they are legible. Stylistic legibility is reinforced by reproducibility, so the process is self-sustaining, helping to explain the way that innovation becomes convention – leading to further innovation in an endlessly recursive process.

Acting, then, is an art of imitation, which is why so many theater makers disassociate themselves from it. In 1996 Jean-Luc Godard griped to the *New York Times* that "actors today just imitate other actors" (*New York Times Magazine*, 53). Godard's beef, like his early modern forebears, is that actors are too apish (zoologists will point out that apes rarely ape). But the Lamarkian model of evolution suggests that actors have no choice but to ape; each actor may adjust the style, alter the inflection, pick up certain mannerisms or discard others, but they are still imitating other actors, as Godard's complaint suggests. In acting, each genotype becomes the phenotype for other actors to copy. The phenotype in every generation is also the genotype – it is what is passed on in every iteration. Thinking about acting without print means thinking about phenotypes not stereotypes.

As an aside, thinking about performance without print means thinking about performance without copyright and intellectual property. Who owned the performances of Richard Burbage or Richard Burton? Some aristocrat in the first instance, some mogul in the second, to whom Richard the first and Richard the second owed their labor. But anyone could mimic Burbage and did according to anecdotes about London toughs who aped his habit of keeping his fingers on his dagger when he played Richard the third.[20] It was, apparently, an early modern meme. (For that matter, Burton's moody muttering left its imprint – without print – on a whole generation of Hollywood chair kickers.) No statute in early English law would allow Burbage to bring action against his imitators. You cannot copyright a gesture since an original gesture is an oxymoron.

This brief digressive suggestion is but to point out that bodies and print pursue radically different memorial programs. Put more crudely, texts and bodies reproduce differently – a proposition that hardly requires expansion. But the central confusion, even collapse, of the terms of print and the terms of performance have confused our understanding of the relationship of print and performance in and after the age of mechanical production. This is nowhere more true than with Shakespeare, the most thoroughly textual (and textualized) form of drama on the modern stage, where the regimes of print have overmastered those of performance. This conclusion ultimately advances a hermeneutics of the handmade, an idea that privileges not regularity and standardization but idiosyncrasy and the quirk. If there is tension between print and performance, this book concludes that that relationship should be more tense. The Shakespearean stage should not only tolerate deviation, it should actively court it.

6.4 Homo digitalis

I will try and avoid "the fool's game of media prophecy" and fall back on the safer one of theatrical prognostication (Raven, 2020: 370). Not much has noticeably changed on the stage since the arrival of digital texts and technologies. Theater is a fundamentally conservative practice, after all, which is why it has such a reputation for liberality. I intend "conservative" in the most strictly root sense: theater invests in the conservation of its practices. (Is this why conservators and mimes both wear white gloves?) The coming of the digital book has not, yet, fundamentally altered the way that actors use these hand tools in the commission of theater. Though it will.

---

[20] In *The Letting of Humour's Blood* Samuel Rowlands describes gallants who would "like Richard the usurper, swagger, / That had his hand continual on his dagger" (1600, A2). He does not specify that this is Burbage, but it is highly likely.

Still, let me reprise and rework this book's opening suggestion: *Everything we know about Shakespeare is preconceived by digitality*. As I argued as I exited "In through the Out Door," however, digital books look a lot like codex, just cooler. The "topology of typography," as El Lissitsky called it in a 1923 manifesto, has not changed that much. Currently, digital books resemble printed books only more tractable and with enhanced storage capacity. The question remains how has or how will digitality cognitively retool us to work differently with text and performance? How will the distinct affordances of digitality, of informational architecture, of the organizational disposition of text and paratext (made so much of here) alter acting? How, in short, will the properties that characterize the born-digital Shakespearean text impact the ways actors "characterize" with, from, through, *via* what Craig Mod calls the "post-artefacutal book" (Raven, 2020: 391)?

"The beeper's going to be making a comeback. Technology's cyclical," Dennis Duffy tells Liz Lemon in an episode from season one of *30 Rock*. It's a great joke and a useful caution against a parallel I'm about to draw between digital and analog interfacing. Reading from a computer or tablet implicates the reader in the physics of the ancient scroll, while reading a book – or codex – implies a movement from left to right and right to left.

This is probably too facile, giving in to the nostalgic allure of the handmade and the armchair comforts of *plus ça change, plus c'est la même chose*. Though we scroll through digital texts, they have affordances that scrolls do not. However insistently you un-pinch print it is not getting any bigger. So the closing question might be how zooming, pinching, and dilating links has and will alter the performance of Shakespeare "from" the digital book. It will, it already has, alter performance in ways that will seem obvious in a decade or two, but are far from apparent at present.

I will close with an insanely optimistic hope that digitality affords above all customization. The digital text is and should be customizable, even bespoke for each consumer. Don't like the line numbers? Turn them off. Glosses getting you down? Make them invisible. Dyslexic? Switch the font from Baskerville to Arial. Is there any harm if every actor customizes their text to the point that everyone is *not* on the same page? It is doubtful. In fact, it might be joyful. Customized texts might introduce diversity, force idiosyncrasy, combat the rationalizations of print, and even push back against the urge to conformity that the per-formatively overdetermined Shakespearean text advances. If nothing else, digital texts might help make Shakespeare weird again, produce irrational performances, unjustified ones, enjoyably idiosyncratic art. We might even disobey the punctuation.

Print tends to even out all the odds, and by reducing the odds, lowering the stakes. Above all, the promise of digitality is that the Shakespearean text might be treated not as liturgy but license. Not prescription but invitation. Not a code but an incitement. There is no meaning *in* the text. The meaning is in us, waiting to be made, waiting for us to make it.

References

Adorno, Theodor (2011) *Quasi una fantasia: Essays on Modern Music*. London: Verso.

The Athenaeum (1905) May 13, 4046.

Barker, Harley Granville (1957) *Plays and Players Magazine*, vol. 4. London: Hansom Books.

Barton, John (1992) *Playing Shakespeare*. New York: Anchor Books.

Baudrillard, Jean (2012) *Impossible Exchange*. London: Verso.

Bergson, Henri (2002) *Key Writings*. New York: Continuum.

Berry, Cicely (2006) *The Actor & the Text*. London: Virgin.

Bristol, Michael (2021) "Character Studies," in Evelyn Gajowski (ed.), *The Arden Research Handbook of Contemporary Shakespeare Criticism*. London: Bloomsbury, 51–66.

Brooks, Douglas A. (2000) *From Playhouse to Printing House: Drama and Authorship in Early Modern England*. Cambridge: Cambridge University Press.

Brown, John Russell (2010) *The Routledge Companion to Directors' Shakespeare*. London: Routledge.

(2012) *The Routledge Companion to Actors' Shakespeare*. London: Routledge.

Clark, William George, and Glover, John (1863) *The Works of William Shakespeare*. 9 vols. Cambridge: Macmillan.

Cloud, Random (1981) "The Psychopathology of Everyday Art," *The Elizabethan Theatre*, 9: 100–168.

Corcoran, Neil (2018) *Reading Shakespeare's Soliloquies: Text, Theatre, and Film*. London: Bloomsbury.

Dawson, Anthony (2005) "The Imaginary Text, or the Curse of the Folio," in W. B. Worthen and Barbra Hodgdon (eds.), *A Companion to Shakespeare and Performance*. Oxford: Blackwell, 141–61.

Day, Barry (2021) *Noël Coward on (and in) Theatre*. New York: Alfred Knopf.

Deleuze, Giles (1973) *Psicanalisi e politica*. Milan: Feltrinelli.

Dyer, Geoff (2021) *See/Saw: Looking at Photographs*. Edinburgh: Canongate Books.

Elam, Keir (2002) *The Semiotics of Theatre and Drama*. London: Routledge.

Erne, Lukas (2008) *Shakespeare's Modern Collaborators*. New York: Continuum.

Forrest, Edwin (c. 1872) *Forrestiana: Anecdotes and Personal Peculiarities of the Great Tragedian*. Folger Shakespeare Library Manuscript B.21.2.

Foster, Hal (2002) *Design and Crime (and Other Diatribes)*. London: Verso.

Freud, Sigmund (1995) *The Basic Writings of Sigmund Freud*. New York: Random House.

Genette, Gérard (1997) *Paratexts: Thresholds of Interpretation*. Cambridge: Cambridge University Press.

Gibson, James L (1966) *The Senses Considered as Perceptual Systems*. London: George Allan & Unwin.

Gikandi, Simon (2012) "The Work of the Book in the Age of Electronic Reproduction," *PMLA*, 127(2): 201–11.

Greenblatt, Stephen, Cohen, Walter, Howard, Jane E., and Eisaman Maus, Katharine (2008) *The Norton Shakespeare*. New York: W. W. Norton.

Greg, W. W. (1942) *The Editorial Problem in Shakespeare: A Survey of the Foundations of the Text*. Oxford: Clarendon Press.

Gross, Roger (2015) *Shakespeare's Verse: A User's Manual for Actors, Directors, Readers, and Enlightened Teachers*. Fayetteville: Pen-L Publishing.

Hall, Peter (2000) *Exposed by the Mask: Form and Language in Drama*. New York: Theatre Communications Group.

Hart, Moss (1959) *Act One: An Autobiography*. New York: St. Martin's Press.

Honigmann, E. A. J. (1996). *Othello*. The Arden Shakespeare. London: Bloomsbury.

Jury, David (2011) *Letterpress: The Allure of the Handmade*. Switzerland: Rotovision.

Kidnie, Margaret J. (2004) "The Staging of Shakespeare's Drama in Print Editions," in Margaret J. Kidnie and Lukas Erne (eds.), *Textual Performances: The Modern Reproduction of Shakespeare's Drama*. Cambridge: Cambridge University Press, 158–77.

Lejeune, Phillipe (1975) *Le pacte autobiographique*. Paris: Seuil.

The Literary Digest (1901) vol. 22.

Loomis, Catherine (2015) "'I Knew by His Face There Was Something in Him': Buried Stage Directions and Authorial Control," in James Knapp (ed.), *Shakespeare and the Power of the Face*. London: Routledge, 115–26.

Machery, Pierre (2006) *A Theory of Literary Production*. Abingdon: Routledge.

Marx, Groucho (1959) *Groucho and Me*. Boston: Da Capo Press.

Masten, Jeffrey (2016) *Queer Philologies: Sex, Language, and Affect in Shakespeare's Time*. Philadelphia: University of Pennsylvania Press.

McInnis, David, and Steggle, Matthew (2014) *Lost Plays in Shakespeare's England*. New York: Palgrave.

Menzer, Paul (2006) "The Actor's Inhibition: Early Modern Acting and the Rhetoric of Restraint," *Renaissance Drama*, 35: 83–112.

Menzer, Paul (2017) *Romeo and Juliet*. London: Bloomsbury.

Ney, Charles (2016) *Directing Shakespeare in America: Current Practices*. London: Bloomsbury.

Norman, Don (2013) *The Design of Everyday Things*. New York: Basic Books.

Orgel, Stephen (2003) *The Authentic Shakespeare, and Other Problems of the Early Modern Stage*. London: Routledge.

Piper, Andrew (2012) "Turning the Page (Roaming, Zooming, Streaming)," in *Book Was There: Reading in Electronic Times*. Chicago: Chicago University Press.

Raven, James (2020) *The Oxford Illustrated History of the Book*. Oxford: Oxford University Press.

Rodenburg, Patsy (2002) *Speaking Shakespeare*. New York: Palgrave.

Schechner, Richard (1985) *Between Theatre and Anthropology*. Philadelphia: University of Pennsylvania Press.

Shapiro, Karl, and Beum, Robert (1965) *A Prosody Handbook*. New York: Harper and Row.

Slater, Ann Pasternak (1982) *Shakespeare the Director*. New York: Prentice Hall.

Smith, Bruce R. (2010) *Phenomenal Shakespeare*. Oxford: Wiley-Blackwell.

Stallybrass, Peter, and DeGrazia, Margreta (1993) "The Materiality of the Shakespearean Text," *Shakespeare Quarterly*, 44: 255–83.

Stanislavski, Konstantin (1995) *An Actor Prepares*. London: Methuen.

Steggle, Matthew (2007) *Laughing and Weeping in Early Modern Theatres*. London: Routledge.

Timpanaro, Sebastiano (1985) *The Freudian Slip: Psychoanalysis and Textual Criticism*. London: Verso.

Tucker, Patrick (1994) *Secrets of Acting Shakespeare: The Original Approach*. London: Routledge.

Watts, Graham (2015) *Shakespeare's Authentic Performance Texts*. Jefferson: McFarland and Company.

Williams, Chris (ed.) (2012) *The Richard Burton Diaries*. New Haven: Yale University Press.

Worthen, W. B. (2005) "Prefixing the Author: Print, Plays, and Performance," in W. B. Worthen and Barbra Hodgdon (eds.), *A Companion to Shakespeare and Performance*. Oxford: Blackwell, 212–30.

(2007) "Performing Shakespeare in Digital Culture," in Robert Shaugnessy (ed.), *The Cambridge Companion to Shakespeare and Popular Culture*. Cambridge: Cambridge University Press, 227–47.

(2014) *Shakespeare Performance Studies*. Cambridge: Cambridge University Press.

Wright, George T. (1988) *Shakespeare's Metrical Art*. Berkeley: University of California Press.

Yachnin, Paul, and Slights, Jessica (2009) *Shakespeare and Character: Theatre, History, Performance, and Theatrical Persons*. New York: Palgrave Macmillan.

Zweig, Stefan (2020) *Encounters and Destinies: A Farewell to Europe*. London: Pushkin Press.

Acknowledgments

Section 1, and this Element in general, was informed and is indebted to many works not directly cited within it. They include but are not limited to W. B. Worthen, *Shakespeare and the Authority of Performance* (1997); Margreta de Grazia and Peter Stallybrass, "The Materiality of the Shakespeare Text," *Shakespeare Quarterly*, 44 (1993); Stephen Orgel, "Acting Scripts, Performing Texts," in *The Authentic Shakespeare, and Other Problems of the Early Modern Stage* (2003); Tiffany Stern, *Documents of Performance in Early Modern England* (2009); Rebecca Schneider, *Performing Remains: Art and War in Times of Theatrical Reenactment* (2011); Paul Werstine, *Early Modern Playhouse Manuscripts and the Editing of Shakespeare* (2012); and Barbara Hodgdon, *Shakespeare, Performance and the Archive* (2015).

Section 4 also owes much to works not cited in its pages. They include Jerome McGann, *The Textual Condition* (1992); Leah Marcus, *Un-Editing the Renaissance: Shakespeare, Marlowe, Milton* (1996); W. B. Worthen, *Print and the Poetics of Modern Drama* (2009); Abigail Rokison, *Shakespearean Verse Speaking* (2010); and Laurie Maguire, *The Rhetoric of the Page* (2021).

Section 6 is much informed by D. A. Brooks, From Playhouse to Printing House: Drama and Authorship in Early Modern England (2000); Julie Stone Peters, Theatre of the Book 1480–1880: Print, Text, and Performance in Europe (2001); Robert Weimann, Author's Pen and Actor's Voice: Playing and Writing in Shakespeare's Theatre (2009); Laurie Maguire, "The Craft of Printing" in David Kastan (ed.), Companion to Shakespeare (2012); Sarah Werner, Studying Early Printed Books, 1450–1800: A Practical Guide (2019); and Claire Bourne, Typographies of Performance in Early Modern England (2020).

Cambridge Elements ≡

Shakespeare Performance

W. B. Worthen
Barnard College

W. B. Worthen is Alice Brady Pels Professor in the Arts, and Chair of the Theatre Department at Barnard College. He is also co-chair of the PhD Program in Theatre at Columbia University, where he is Professor of English and Comparative Literature.

Cambridge Elements ☰

Shakespeare Performance

Printed in the United States
by Baker & Taylor Publisher Services